BUON APPETITO

Jordan Morello

THE FIT BODY

Table of Contents

A Little About Me

When I posted my first #buonappetito video on Instagram, I never imagined it would lead me to writing this book. When it all started, I was just having fun in my kitchen, most of the time cooking with mama dukes. Mama dukes Is my mom so if you ever hear me say that, that's who I'm referring too. There is a great story that comes with that name but I'll tell you at another time.

When I first started posting recipes, I just wanted a way to show others that cooking can be fun and not only fun but easy as well! I got into cooking at a young age and really started to get into it when I was in college. Well when you live alone you have to learn how to cook, the easy mac and hot dogs just wasn't cutting it anymore... It's funny because as I posted more and more of course more criticism comes with the territory and I had some of my friends and even family saying how goofy I was, "maybe you should be a bit more professional" ... Ehhh No... haha. I know I'm a goofy, crazy guy... That's the way I am, that's how I'm staying. I struggled with self-identity for a while throughout my life. I always knew who I wanted to become although it's easy to be talked out of a certain idea by those closest to you. If anyone has anything to say to you just remember to stay true to yourself!

I saw every video as an opportunity to share a new recipe with someone who may be struggling with nutrition or just to teach someone how to cook. I wanted to show anyone that would watch my crazy videos that cooking can be fun, easy and delicious! Also, it doesn't have to cost a ton of money!

When it comes to cooking, mama dukes taught me so much throughout my childhood. Some of my friends who would eat dinners at my house know that my Mom does not mess around in the kitchen. She would work all day and come home and still cook giant feasts for her family and anyone else who would show up... So when I was in high school that's where I started to help out in the kitchen and watch what my mom did. I started using the techniques myself and fell in love with cooking.

Cooking and nutrition are such a huge aspect in my life, it has completely changed my life and taught me the benefits first hand not only physically but mentally and soulfully!

Having adhd and tourrettes is not an easy task when going through school... medication makes you feel like a zombie and you're always being taken into the smaller classes for "extra time" ... Its not great for confidence but because of my new found love of nutrition and exercise at a young age, I was able to quit the medication and persevere. I owe everything I've worked for to nutrition and exercise, the lessons learned and the benefits gained are incomparable.

My approach to health is all about making small lifestyle changes, not huge leaps but instead following a sustainable, non-restrictive and flexible plan. In fact, my diet is pretty shocking at times. I mean, if you know me you definitely see what I can put down... I've always trained hard but when I was young, I never truly took nutrition seriously.

In college I often ate peanut butter jelly, cookies, cereal, mac n cheese. Most of these foods often left me feeling sluggish and tired... I would then just drink up more caffeinated drinks in between class and training clients so keeping a lean-fit physique was kind of out of the question in those years. I was always focused on size when I was in school and wanted to be the biggest, strongest kid around campus. I realized how dumb that truly was and I slowly figured out no matter how hard you train you won't be able to outwork a bad diet.

I started to really study nutrition in my junior year of college at University of Central Florida, I studied Health Sciences Pre-Medical and Minored in Sports and Exercise Science. I realized just how important real whole foods are for my energy levels and making changes to my body. The more I understood, the more I began to transform my own body and I was able to be a better trainer to my clients. At this time, I began to really find my love for helping others through nutrition and exercise. I saw the benefits and experienced them first hand myself, and I needed to share this with others.

After graduation, I was working in the hospital collecting volunteer hours for medical school. I started shadowing orthopedic surgeries and these were long days and hours... sometimes only seeing 2-3 patients. In my head I just knew that I wanted to help others and leave my mark on the masses; I wanted to help more people. This was the time social media started to really come around and be popular so I started posting workout videos, food pictures and of course speedo modeling photos (to help grow my audience of course). I began to share more and more content out on the internet until I was approached by Men's Fitness magazine and Muscle & Fitness. They flew me up to New York City where I did my first photo shoot, got a full video workout series and spread in their magazine! I started to gain some traction and got some notoriety online, then I would receive messages from others asking me certain questions about my workout plan, nutrition and telling me all about the shocking info they've received from other professionals. I realized how shocking the fitness and nutrition industries are and the mumbo jumbo information they can spread to these poor individuals. It's sad to see when someone is trying to make life changes, there is so much wrong information out there, you just don't know who to trust. That's why I don't believe in these fad diets out there or these crazy 6 day to six-pack routines or the amount of diet products that are out there. People have been convinced that the only way to truly lose weight is by doing these extreme weight loss approaches by taking diet products and cutting calories drastically which in reality creates these huge energy deficits and only leads to yo-yo diets, weight loss and gain.

At the beginning of this year January 2020, I took the plunge and created my very own online nutrition and training app to help educate people properly and save them from these damaging fad diets and wrongful training plans. My goal is to create a custom sustainable meal plan with foods my clients enjoy and love eating the most. Along with showing them how to properly train and ensure they receive the results they deserve. Every client of mine gets a custom nutrition plan and custom workout plan tailored to their body, their goals and the results they are looking to accomplish. My goal is to help millions of people throughout my life time and truly leave my mark. I want to be known for the love, support and knowledge I was able to share while changing others' lives for the better. I know nothing happens overnight and I'm okay with that, but as long as I'm here, I will continue to make a difference in people's lives one by one.

Well, that's a little about me and my story of how this book came to fruition. I am very excited to share my knowledge and recipes with you. I hope you enjoy the book and get inspired to have fun in the kitchen.

Love,

Jordan Morello
The Fit Body

What's Cooking Good Looking

Why Diet's Don't Work!

The problem with going on a "diet" is that they just don't work, well at least not in the long term. Absolutely, you can lose weight initially because of the drastic decrease in calories but the likelihood you will soon return to your old eating habits is very likely. Then you'll be back to gaining the weight you lost, motivation begins to lack and most individuals give up because they didn't see the results they set out to achieve. Working with 100's of clients has only taught me one thing, success only happens when your routine is enjoyable and most importantly sustainable. A meal plan needs to be easy to follow, filled with foods you actually enjoy eating and most importantly stress free. Life is stressful enough and getting healthy and fit should be the one thing that alleviates those concerns from your life. Nobody wants to spend countless hours in the kitchen everyday.

That's why I wanted to create The Fit Body Program. I know we all live busy lives, but no matter how busy you are, You always have to make time for your health. Take control of your life, find 20 minutes to cook for yourself and cut out 30 minutes to do some daily exercise. I wanted to create this cookbook to show you some of my favorite meals I enjoy cooking and still get amazing results while living a busy life. I want to teach you how to fuel your body the correct way, feel energized and look good! This all starts in the kitchen, no matter how much you exercise, you will not out work a bad diet. Trust me... I've tried.

Most of the recipes in my book are quick, easy to cook and delicious! I wanted to show you how to cook, why to cook and how fun cooking can actually be. An easy way to prep for yourself is by making double of each portion sizing to make sure you are covered for your meals in the following day! That is if you are a meal prepper! The busier lifestyle you live, the more you will need to prep your meals! So when you find a few favorites of these recipes prep them up for a few days ahead of time to ensure your success!

THERE ARE NO SHORTCUTS TO SUCCESS

If I can teach you anything it's this... I want you to ignore the fat burning ads, supplements, meal replacements and juice diets. Those diets are not solutions in any way, they are part of the problem. These go against some of the most basic principles of nutrition and what our bodies use as fuel to function at our optimal levels. Instead, I want you to focus on eating more food! Yes I just said that! I'm not sure where we went wrong in the industry of fitness and nutrition but it seems that everyone has a new found fear that carbs could possibly kill them... or at least make them fat. I mean, you could rob a bank with a bagel in LA... We are going to focus on eating whole, nutritious foods and most importantly actually enjoy what we are eating while getting results! Listen, there are no shortcuts when it comes to creating a fit body... It takes time, dedication and consistency through the right nutrition and exercise practice. Listen to your body, enjoy your journey and most importantly have fun. This is your fit body.

MACRONUTRIENTS, WHAT THE HECK ARE THOSE?!

Alright, so our main energy sources come from fats, proteins and carbohydrates which we call Macronutrients. Each of these play a very important role in helping our bodies stay strong, healthy and fit. This book is filled with all different recipes that will nourish your body with all 3 of these and won't cut these out like some diets out there.

LET'S BREAK DOWN FATS

Many people try to avoid fat in their diets, the word "FAT" is terrifying because we automatically think "weight gain". Although fats play such an important role by providing our bodies with an important source of energy at times of starvation or in a caloric deprivation. Fats are usually the first thing that people start to cut out when trying to lose weight, but not all fats are created equally. Some fats are trans fats which are found in processed foods and should be avoided. Other fats are essential for our bodies, such as omega-3s (found In oily fish) which help rid our bodies of inflammation. Fat also plays an essential role in vitamin absorptions in our body.

What's The Deal With Protein?

Protein provides our bodies with building blocks (amino acids) for muscle and other important structures such as the brain, nervous system, blood, skin and hair. Many of my recipes contain protein sources from eggs, fish, chicken, beef and turkey which are considered complete protein sources because they all carry essential amino acids. If you are vegetarian, an easy switch would be adding tofu, lentils or tempeh instead of using animal protein. Although in order to get the amount of protein needed to fuel your body you may need to eat much larger portion sizes.

SHOULD I TAKE PROTEIN POWDER?

This is the biggest question I get as a trainer, should I take a protein powder in addition to my meals.

I always say to stick with real whole foods not a powder to burn fat and build a lean physique. Supplements are great, but they are not to be confused as a meal replacement. They are called "supplements" for a reason, which act as an addition to your already complete nutritious meal plan. You will see in some of my recipes like protein balls, I use protein powder. Whey protein is an amazing post-workout addition to your diet beause it helps replenish the muscle quickly and gives your body an ample amount of essential amino acids to begin repairing and rebuilding muscle. There are so many incredible non-dairy powders out there as well, so if you are lactose intolerant or vegetarian, I would look for a vegan, hemp or even pea protein powder. I've taken plant based protein for awhile now and have no digestive issues ever!

OKAY, BUT WHAT ABOUT CARBOHYDRATES?

Okay, the one we have all been waiting for... drum roll please! Carbs! There is so much confusion when it comes to carbohydrates, which ones are good, which are bad and when you can and can't eat them. First and foremost, carbohydrates are an incredible energy source and can truly transform your physique. Im sure we all have heard that eating carbohydrates around bed time can make you fat. That's not true and I've been eating oatmeal before bed for years, but that's a story for another time! Carbohydrates don't make you fat, what makes you fat is when we over eat and put our bodies into a caloric surplus. Meaning, that we are consuming more calories then expending energy. So eating the correct amount and tracking your macronutrients can ensure burning more fat and creating a more lean fit body. Carbohydrates are the bodies main source of energy, especially during rigorous exercise. Carbs are needed to aid in proper function of the central nervous system, kidneys and muscles. Carbs also contain fiber which aids in a healthy digestive system. The list goes on although not all carbs are created equal!

When choosing your carbs, try your best to steer clear of white carbohydrates which can have a high glycemic load. Meaning more white bread, pasta, rice can turn into sugar and be stored in our body as excess fat. These foods can be very beneficial after an intense workout although most of the time I would vouch for the brown rice or the sweet potato.

LETS GET COOKING!

Okay, hopefully you a have a better understanding of macronutrients and how you are going to use them to fuel your body the proper way! No more fad diets, low calories and cutting carbs for you! It's time to enjoy the foods you eat, feel full of energy and transform into a lean cooking machine!

In this book, you will see a ton of different variety recipes I have created for you! I love creating different options because I mean really how many different way's can you spin a piece of chicken! When you come across one of your favorite meals, one of the best things to do is cook double so you can prep for the next day or two! It's preparing for your success, that way you are not tempted to go out, spend money and eat something that may not be the healthiest!

These recipes were designed to be fun, easy, quick and delicious! I am no Michelin star chef, but boy do I love to cook! It's easy to fall in love and enjoy cooking when the recipes are enjoyable to cook! That's why I put together some of my favorite recipes for you in this book! 100 Recipes from snacks, sides, breakfast, lunch, dinner and more! I hope you enjoy this book and most importantly have fun cooking.

Buon Appetito!

Jordan Morello

Dedicated To My Favorite Ingredient

My mom is by far one of the biggest influences in my life. Without her this book, my mission and what I do would not be possible. She has been there for me every step of my life, every failure, every set back, every success and good time. No matter what she is there giving me the most support, love and optimistic attitude to accomplish whatever I set my mind on. Even the days when she is not feeling her best, she is always there uplifting me and sharing her love. I am so blessed to have the mother I have. Mom, because of you my dreams were made possible. I love you so much. Here's to many more memories, books and adventures.

snacks

No Bake Protein Balls

PREPARATION **15 Minutes** TOTAL **45 Minutes** YIELD **12 Servings**

INGREDIENTS

- 1.5 scoops protein powder
- 1.5 cups whole rolled oats
- 1 cup natural peanut butter
- 1 teaspoon vanilla extract
- ¼ cup maple syrup
- ¾ cup lily's chocolate chips

DIRECTION

» In a mixing bowl, add all ingredients to bowl. Mix it on up! With your hands roll mixture into 12 separate balls on parchment paper. Place in Fridge for 30 minutes.

Buon Appetito!

Homemade Peanut Butter

PREPARATION **10 Minutes** TOTAL **10 Minutes** YIELD **3 Cups**

INGREDIENTS

- 3 cups dry roasted peanuts (salted or unsalted)

DIRECTION

» Place peanuts into a medium food processor or blender. Mix it on up until the mixture is very smooth, stop every 30 seconds to scrape the sides of the blender down towards the blender. First glance the mixture will be thick. Repeat this for about 8 minutes! The Peanuts will then become smooth and creamy!

Buon Appetito!

Homemade Granola

PREPARATION **10 Minutes** | TOTAL **40 Minutes** | YIELD **4-6**

INGREDIENTS

2 cups whole rolled oats

1/3 cup maple syrup

2 teaspoons cinnamon

2 tablespoons creamy almond butter

1 teaspoon vanilla extract

Optional add ins (cranberries, chopped almonds, coconut flakes)

DIRECTION

» Preheat oven to 300°F, line baking sheet with parchment paper. Mix all ingredients together in a small bowl until smooth! Spread mixture on parchment paper and bake for 25-30 minutes.

Buon Appetito!

Holy Moley Guacomole

PREPARATION **10 Minutes** | TOTAL **10 Minutes** | YIELD **4-6**

INGREDIENTS

3 ripe avocados

¼ cup diced onion & cilantro

2 limes juiced

1 small japapeno

Salt & Pepper to taste

DIRECTION

» In a large bowl, combine the avocados, onion, cilantro, lime juice, jalapeno and salt, pepper. Mash the mixture until the ingredients are chunky & delicious! Season with a dash of cumin!

Buon Appetito!

Homemade Hummus

🗓 PREPARATION
5 Minutes
⏱ TOTAL
5 Minutes
🍴 YIELD
8

INGREDIENTS

1 ½ cups chickpeas,
drained and rinsed
2 tablespoons tahini
2 tablespoons olive oil
2 tablespoons lemon juice
1 garlic clove
½ cup water or as needed to blend

DIRECTION

» In a food processor or blender, place all
ingredients into blender and blend until
very smooth. Add water as needed while
blending to desired consistency. Plate the
hummus and add (optional) paprika, red
pepper flakes or parsley to garnish!

Buon Appetito!

Crispy Cinnamon Apple Chips

PREPARATION
5 Minutes

TOTAL
1 hour 5 Minutes

YIELD
4

INGREDIENTS

4 gala apples

2 tablespoons cinnamon

2 teaspoons coconut sugar

DIRECTION

» Preheat oven to 350ºF. Slice apples thinly. In a large bowl toss apples with sugar and cinnamon. Place apples on baking sheet and bake for 1 hour check occasionally to flip.

Buon Appetito!

Prosciutto Wrapped Arugula

🥄 PREPARATION
10 Minutes ⏱ TOTAL (BAKE TIME) **10 Minutes** 🍴 YIELD **20**

INGREDIENTS

20 paper-thin slices prosciutto

4 cups fresh baby arugula

Truffle oil

Balsamic glaze

Parmigiano Reggiano Cheese

DIRECTION

» Take your paper-thin slice of prosciutto and lay it down on a cutting board. Grab a few arugula leaves and place them at the end of your prosciutto slice. Drizzle truffle oil, balsamic glaze, salt & pepper on top. Top the arugula with Parmigiano cheese. Roll the arugula and prosciutto until you have a perfect wrap.

Buon Appetito!

Tomato
Goat-Cheese
Toast

PREPARATION
10 Minutes

TOTAL
10 Minutes

YIELD
10

INGREDIENTS

1 loaf Italian bread

6 ounces goat cheese

2 plum tomatoes

2 tablespoons olive oil

2 cloves garlic minced

2 tablespoons chopped parsley

DIRECTION

» Preheat the oven to 400°F. In a small bowl stir together goat cheese, parsley. In a medium bowl mix together the chopped tomatoes, garlic, olive oil, parsley, salt & pepper. Slice bread into small ½ inch thick pieces and place on a baking tin. Toast for 5 minutes. Spread cheese mixture on top of toast and top with tomato mixture.

Buon Appetito!

Crispy Roasted Chickpeas

PREPARATION **5 Minutes**   TOTAL **20 Minutes**   YIELD **2**

INGREDIENTS

1 ½ cups cooked chickpeas, drained and rinsed

Extra Virgin Olive Oil

Sea Salt

Paprika

Curry Powder

DIRECTION

» Preheat oven to 400°F. Line a large baking sheet with parchment paper. In a small bowl mix olive oil, sea salt, paprika and curry powder together. Then add in your chickpeas and softly toss them in the mixture. Place on your baking sheet and roast the chickpeas for 15 minutes. Remove from oven, add a dash of sea salt on top.

Buon Appetito!

No Bake Granola Bar

PREPARATION **5 Minutes**   TOTAL (CHILLING TIME) **60 Minutes**   YIELD **8**

INGREDIENTS

1 cup smooth natural peanut butter

2/3 cup honey or maple syrup

1 teaspoon vanilla extract

2 ½ cups whole rolled oats

1/3 cup lily's chocolate chips

DIRECTION

» Line a baking pan with parchment paper. In a large bowl stir the peanut butter, honey, vanilla and salt until smooth. Fold in the oats and chocolate chips and mix it on up. Add the mixture into your baking pan, pressing firmly to flatten the mixture out. Pop in the fridge and chill for 1 hour, slice it on up.

Buon Appetito!

Get Your Greens Smoothie

PREPARATION **5 Minutes**   TOTAL **5 Minutes**   YIELD **1**

INGREDIENTS

1 cup almond milk

2 cups spinach

1 ripe banana

1 cup pineapple chunks

1 cup ice

DIRECTION

» Take all your beautiful ingredients and throw them in your blender. Blend it on up! Pour into a small glass.

Buon Appetito!

sides

Roasted Brussels Sprouts

PREPARATION
5 Minutes

TOTAL
35 Minutes

YIELD
3-4

INGREDIENTS

1 lb brussels sprouts

Extra virgin olive oil

1 tablespoon lemon juice

¼ cup parmesan cheese (grated)

1 tablespoon fresh thyme leaves

Parsley leaves

Red pepper flakes

DIRECTION

» Preheat oven to 425ºF Line a baking sheet with parchment paper and place brussel sprouts on top. Drizzle olive oil, salt, pepper and red pepper flakes on top of the sprouts. Roast for 30 minutes or until golden brown. Toss sprouts with the lemon juice, parmesan and thyme leaves. Garnish with parsley and red pepper flakes.

Buon Appetito!

Stuffed Mushrooms

⌇ PREPARATION
20 Minutes ⏱ TOTAL
40 Minutes 🍴 YIELD
20

INGREDIENTS

20 medium white mushrooms
(stems removed)

2 ounces goat cheese

¼ chopped roasted red pepper

5 ounces chopped spinach

1 ½ cups breadcrumbs

DIRECTION

» Preheat oven to 375°F. Place mushrooms on a baking sheet
with a dash of olive oil spread across the sheet. Grab a food
processor and combine the goat cheese, red pepper, spinach,
breadcrumbs, salt and pepper. Mix it on up! Stuff each
mushroom with a heaping spoonful of your mixture. Top and
sprinkle the remaining breadcrumbs on top of the mushrooms.
Bake the mushrooms for 20 minutes.

Buon Appetito!

Cajun Sweet Potatoes

⌇ PREPARATION
10 Minutes ⏱ TOTAL (BAKE TIME)
60 Minutes 🍴 YIELD
4

INGREDIENTS

4 sweet potatoes (8 oz each)

1 garlic bulb

1 teaspoon cajun spice

¾ Greek yogurt

4 scallions

DIRECTION

» Preheat oven to 350°F. Rinse potatoes and then slice into 1 inch
thick rounds. Place in an oven safe pan with the whole garlic
bulb. Toss in 1 tablespoon of coconut oil, red wine vinegar, salt,
pepper and cajun spice. Roast potatoes for 1 hour until soft and
carmelized. Once out of the oven, plate the potatoes on top of
the Greek yogurt. Finely chop up your scallions and sprinkle on
top of the potatoes.

Buon Appetito!

Muffin Tin Potatoes Au Gratin

PREPARATION 10 Minutes **TOTAL** 45 Minutes **YIELD** 12

INGREDIENTS

2 large potatoes
(peeled & thinly sliced)

2 tablespoons butter

3 cloves garlic

2 tablespoons flour

¾ cup almond milk

½ cup parmesan cheese (grated)

DIRECTION

» Preheat oven to 400°F In a saucepan over heat butter over medium heat. Add in garlic and stir for about a minute. Then add in flour to garlic mixture and allow to thicken for 2 minutes. Slowly take off the heat and pour almond milk into the mixture and whisk until smooth and thickened. Add in parmesan cheese, salt and pepper to taste. Divide sliced potatoes into each muffin tin evenly and top with cheese sauce. Bake potatoes for 30 minutes!

Buon Appetito!

Roasted Garlic Potatoes

 **PREPARATION** 10 Minutes **TOTAL (BAKE TIME)** 45 Minutes **YIELD** 4

INGREDIENTS

1 ½ lbs small red or white potatoes (cut into quarters)

2 tablespoons extra virgin olive oil

2 garlic cloves (minced)

1 lemon (juiced)

3 tablespoons parsley

DIRECTION

» Preheat oven to 375ºF In a large bowl add potatoes, olive oil, lemon juice, salt, pepper, garlic and toss until the potatoes are well coated. Spray a baking sheet with non-stick cooking spray. Roast Potatoes for 45 minutes, flipping occasionally. Remove potatoes and top with lemon juice.

Buon Appetito!

Roasted Butternut Squash

PREPARATION 10 Minutes **TOTAL** 40 Minutes **YIELD** 4

INGREDIENTS

1 butternut squash peeled, seeds scooped and cubed
Extra virgin olive oil
Sea salt and fresh ground black pepper
Chopped parsley

DIRECTION

» Preheat oven to 400°F Peel and scoop butternut squash and chop into cubes. Place on a baking sheet and line with parchment paper. Drizzle olive oil, sea salt and pepper on top. Roast squash for 30 minutes or until golden brown. Sprinkle chopped parsley on top.

Buon Appetito!

Cilantro Lime Rice

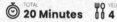

PREPARATION 5 Minutes **TOTAL** 20 Minutes **YIELD** 4

INGREDIENTS

1 cup long grain jasmine rice
1 ½ cups of water
3 teaspoons extra virgin olive oil
1 small garlic clove (minced)
2 scallions (chopped)
2 tablespoons lime juice
½ cup cilantro (chopped)
¼ red pepper flakes
& jalepeno (diced)

DIRECTION

» In a sauce pan over medium heat combine rice, water and 1 teaspoon of olive oil. Bring to a boil, cover and allow to simmer for 20 minutes. Fluff rice, allow to sit for 1 minute to cool. Then add in 2 remaining teaspoons olive oil, garlic, scallions, lime juice, cilantro, red pepper flakes, jalepeno, salt and pepper! Mix it on up.

Buon Appetito!

Honey Roasted Carrots

PREPARATION
10 Minutes

TOTAL
45 Minutes

YIELD
6

INGREDIENTS

- 1/4 cup butter
- 2 tbsp honey
- 1/2 teaspoon rosemary
- 20 carrots peeled and halved
- Fresh Thyme
- Salt & Pepper

DIRECTION

» Preheat the oven to 400°F. In a sauce pan over low heat melt down butter. Stir in honey, rosemary, season with garlic powder, salt and pepper. Place Carrots on a large baking sheet, drizzle glaze on top of carrots and toss until well coated. Roast for 34-40 minutes. Season with fresh thyme and serve!

Buon Appetito!

Sweet Mandarin Rice

PREPARATION **25 Minutes** TOTAL **30 Minutes** YIELD **6**

INGREDIENTS

3/4 cup uncooked long grain rice

1/3 cup raisins

2 tablespoons butter or margarine

1/2 teaspoon nutmeg

2 tablespoons honey

1/3 cup sliced almonds, toasted

1 (11 ounce) can mandarin orange segments, drained

DIRECTION

» Cook rice according to package directions. Stir in raisins, butter, nutmeg and honey. Cook over medium heat, stirring occasionally, until heated through (3 to 5 minutes). Gently stir in almonds and oranges; let stand 1 minute to heat through.

Buon Appetito!

Maple Cornbread Muffins

⚙ PREPARATION
10 Minutes　◷ TOTAL **30 Minutes**　🍴 YIELD **9–10**

INGREDIENTS

1 cup cornmeal

1 cup flour

2 teaspoons baking powder

2 tablespoons rosemary (chopped)

¾ cup unsweetened almond milk

½ cup maple syrup

½ cup coconut oil

DIRECTION

» Preheat oven to 350°F In a large bowl add in cornmeal, flour, baking powder. In a small bowl whisk together all wet ingredients and fold into the dry. Mix it on up and fill the muffin tins with the mixture. Bake the muffins for 20 minutes. Allow the muffins to cool and finish them off with the rosemary flakes on top.

Buon Appetito!

Oven-Roasted Vegetables

PREPARATION 10 Minutes **TOTAL** 40 Minutes **YIELD** 4

INGREDIENTS

- 1 medium zucchini
- 1 medium summer squash
- 1 medium red bell pepper
- 1 medium yellow bell pepper
- 1 lb fresh asparagus
- 1 medium red onion
- 3 tablespoons extra virgin olive oil

DIRECTION

» Preheat oven to 450°F Cut all vegetables and place into a large roasting pan. Toss the vegetable in olive oil, salt and pepper. Spread vegetables into a single layer and roast for 30 minutes or until golden brown. Mix Occasionally and Serve.

Buon Appetito!

salads

Watermelon Feta Salad

PREPARATION 15 Minutes **TOTAL** 15 Minutes **YIELD** 4

INGREDIENTS

5 cups watermelon (cubed)

1 avocado (cubed)

1 cup english cucumber

¼ cup red onion (thinly sliced)

1/3 cup feta cheese

1/3 cup mint or basil leaves

½ jalepeno (thinly sliced)

2 tablespoons olive oil

3 tablespoons lime juice

1 teaspoon sea salt

½ garlic clove (minced)

DIRECTION

» In a small bowl whisk together the olive oil, lime juice, garlic and sea salt. Place the watermelon, cucumber and red onions on a large platter. Drizzle half the dressing over the platter. Then top with the avocado, mint and jalapeno pepper. Drizzle remaining dressing and serve.

Buon Appetito!

Broccoli Salad

🔪 PREPARATION
10 Minutes ⏱ TOTAL **25 Minutes** 🍴 YIELD **4-6**

INGREDIENTS

3 tablespoons extra virgin olive oil

3 tablespoons mayo

1 ½ tablespoons apple cider vinegar

2 teaspoons Dijon mustard

1 garlic clove (minced)

1/3 cup red onion (diced)

1/3 cup dried cranberries

½ cup almonds

½ cup pumpkin seeds

1 tablespoon soysauce

½ teaspoon maple syrup

¼ paprika

DIRECTION

» Preheat oven to 350ºF Grab a baking sheet and line with parchment paper. Chop the broccoli into ½ inch pieces. In a large bowl whisk together the olive oil, mayo, mustard, apple cider vinegar, maple syrup, garlic and salt. Add and toss the broccoli, onions and cranberries in the sauce. Place the almonds and pumpkin seeds on the baking sheet, toss with maple syrup, soy sauce and paprika. Roast the almonds for 15 minutes. Remove and cool for 5 minutes! Toss the almonds into the salad and serve.

Buon Appetito!

Black Bean Tomato Quinoa Salad

PREPARATION **10 Minutes**   TOTAL **25 Minutes**   YIELD **4**

INGREDIENTS

1 ½ cups Quinoa

2 Tablespoons white balsamic vinegar

3 Tablespoons olive oil

2 tablespoons melted butter

1 teaspoon sugar (optional)

1 15 oz can black beans

2 medium tomatoes, diced (or use cherry tomatoes)

2 green onions, chopped

1/3 cup fresh cilantro or parsley, chopped

DIRECTION

» Bring 3 cups of water to a boil. Add quinoa, reduce heat and allow to simmer for 15 minutes. In a small bowl add the vinegar, oil, butter. Take quinoa off heat. Add mixture into quinoa and mix it on up. Then add the beans, tomatoes, onions, cilantro, salt and pepper to taste. Place in large bowl can be served hot or cold.

Buon Appetito!

Blackened Shrimp and Quinoa Bowl

PREPARATION
20 Minutes · TOTAL **25-30 Minutes** · YIELD **2**

INGREDIENTS

1 cup quinoa

10-12 shrimp, peeled and deveined

1 tablespoon Cajun seasoning

1 tablespoon olive oil

1 tablespoon unsalted butter

4 cups arugula
(and/or spring greens)

2 tablespoons goat cheese

2 tangerines (or orange segments)

1 medium avocado, pitted, peeled,
and cut lengthwise into slices

Citrus vinaigrette:

1 small shallot, finely chopped

¾ cup olive oil

3 tablespoon fresh lemon juice

2 tablespoon fresh orange juice

¼ teaspoon finely grated lemon zest

Kosher salt and freshly ground
pepper to taste

DIRECTION

» Bring 2 cups water to a boil in a saucepan with tight fitting lid. Add quinoa to boiling water and reduce to simmer. Allow to cook undisturbed for 15 minutes. While quinoa is cooking, sauté shrimp in the olive oil, butter and Cajun seasoning until nicely charred and opaque throughout, 2-3 minutes on each side.

» To make the dressing, in a small bowl, combine the shallot, oil, lemon juice, orange juice and lemon zest. Season with sea salt and black pepper, whisk to blend.

» In a large bowl, combine the arugula and or field greens and toss with tablespoon of vinaigrette. Transfer the salad greens to a large shallow bowl or platter or 2 individual bowls. Arrange the shrimp, tangerine segments and avocado on top with tablespoon of goat cheese in the center. Drizzle the rest of the vinaigrette on top and serve.

Buon Appetito!

Greek Salad

PREPARATION 15 Minutes **TOTAL** 15 Minutes **YIELD** 4

INGREDIENTS

1 English cucumber

1 green bell pepper

2 cups cherry tomatoes

5 ounces feta cheese

1/3 cup red onion

1/3 cup kalamata olives

1/3 cup mint leave

Dressing

¼ cup extra virgin olive oil

3 tablespoons red wine vinegar

1 garlic clove (minced)

½ teaspoon dried oregano

¼ teaspoon Dijon mustard

DIRECTION

» In a small bowl whisk together the olive oil, vinegar, oregano, mustard, salt and pepper. Grab a large platter, spread the cucumber, green pepper, cherry tomatoes, feta cheese, red onions and olives. Drizzle with the dressing and toss. Season with a bit more salt, pepper and oregano.

Buon Appetito!

Italian Chopped Salad

PREPARATION
15 Minutes

TOTAL
15 Minutes

YIELD
6

INGREDIENTS

1 small head iceberg lettuce

1 head radicchio

½ small red onion (thinly sliced)

1 pint cherry tomatoes (halved)

1 can chickpeas

4 ounces fresh mozzarella

4 ounces provolone cheese (diced)

5 pepperoncini (sliced)

Lemon Vinaigrette Ingredients

¼ cup extra virgin olive oil

1 ½ tablespoons lemon juice

1 tablespoon red wine vinegar

½ shallot (chopped)

1 garlic clove (minced)

DIRECTION

» In a small bowl whisk together the olive oil, lemon juice, vinegar, shallot, garlic, oregano, salt and pepper. Cut the iceberg lettuce in half, cut the core of the lettuce out. Slice the lettuce in small strips and repeat with the radicchio. In a large salad bowl combine the lettuce, radicchio, tomatoes, chickpeas, mozzarella, provolone, and pepperoncini. Drizzle the dressing over the salad and toss. Season with a bit more salt and pepper.

Buon Appetito!

Cucumber Salad

PREPARATION **10 Minutes** TOTAL **15 Minutes** YIELD **4**

INGREDIENTS

1 English cucumber

2 tablespoons rice vinegar

½ tablespoon agave or honey

1/3 cup red onion

¼ teaspoon sesame oil

1 tablespoon chopped dill

1 tablespoon fresh mint leaves

DIRECTION

» Grab yourself a large bowl, combine the vinegar, agave, cucumber, onion, sesame oil, dill and salt. Toss the salad and chill it for 10 minutes in the refrigerator. Top the salad with fresh mint.

Buon Appetito!

Mediterranean Chickpea Salad

PREPARATION 20 Minutes **TOTAL** 20 Minutes **YIELD** 4-6

INGREDIENTS

3 cucumbers

2 cups cooked chickpeas

1 cup cherry tomatoes

2 tablespoons extra virgin olive oil

3 garlic cloves (minced)

2 tablespoon lemon juice

1 ½ teaspoon cumin

1 teaspoon salt

1/3 cup chopped roasted red peppers

¼ cup finely chopped parsley

3 ounces goat cheese

¼ cup fresh mint

DIRECTION

» Grab a large bowl and combine the olive oil, garlic, lemon juice, cumin, salt and pepper. Grab a small skillet and over medium heat, cook the chickpeas for 5-7 minutes. In a large bowl add the chickpeas, tomatoes, cucumbers, red pepper and parsley. Drizzle the dressing over the large bowl and toss. Transfer the salad onto a platter and serve with a dollop of goat cheese and mint.

Buon Appetito!

Easy-Peasy Mediterranean Pasta Salad

PREPARATION **10 Minutes**   TOTAL **10 Minutes**   YIELD **6**

INGREDIENTS

3 cups rotini pasta
2 cups cherry tomatoes
2 cups arugula
1 cucumber
1 cup chickpeas
1 cup feta cheese
1 cup basil
1 teaspoon salt
½ cup parsley
½ cup chopped mint
¼ cup pine nuts

Dressing

¼ cup extra virgin olive oil
1 teaspoon Dijon mustard
3 tablespoons lemon juice
3 garlic cloves
¼ teaspoon
red pepper flakes

DIRECTION

» In a large pot bring water to boil. Cook the rotini pasta until al dente. While the pasta cooks, in a small bowl whisk together the olive oil, lemon juice, mustard, garlic, red pepper flakes and salt. Drain the pasta and toss with olive oil and allow the pasta to cool at room temperature. Add the pasta to a large bowl and add the tomatoes, chickpeas, arugula, cucumbers, feta cheese, basil, parsley, mint and pine nuts. Drizzle the dressing over and toss everything together. Season with salt, pepper.
Buon Appetito!

soups

Moroccan Chicken Stew

PREPARATION **20 Minutes** TOTAL **60 Minutes** YIELD **4**

INGREDIENTS

1 tablespoon vegetable oil

4 skinless chicken breasts, cubed

1 chopped medium onion

Chopped garlic –
about 2 tablespoons

1 teaspoon each:
Salt, cinnamon, cumin,
curry powder, ground ginger

Crushed red pepper flakes
(for very spicy ` less for mild)

2, 14 ½ oz. cans of stewed tomatoes

4 medium potatoes
cut into 1 inch pieces (about 2 lbs)

1 cup baby carrots

½ cup raisins

2 tablespoons lemon juice

DIRECTION

» Heat oil. Add chicken and brown
on all sides. Remove chicken from
pot and set aside. In the same pot,
cook and stir onions and garlic
until onions are translucent. Stir
in all seasonings for 30 seconds
or until fragrant. Add tomatoes,
potatoes, carrots and raisins. Heat
until tomatoes just come to a boil
(mixture will look dry at first, but
additional liquid will for as stew
cooks). Return chicken to pot and
cover tightly. Reduce heat and
simmer 35-45 minutes or until
vegetables are tender. Stir in lemon
juice just before serving.

Buon Appetito!

Lentil and Vegetable Soup

PREPARATION **15 Minutes** TOTAL **30 Minutes** YIELD **4**

INGREDIENTS

1 tablespoon olive oil

2/3 cup diced celery

½ cup diced white onions

1/3 cup diced carrots

3 tablespoons diced shallots

2 teaspoons minced garlic

2 quarts vegetable stock (or broth)

1 ¼ cup dry brown lentils

2 teaspoons whole-grain mustard

2 teaspoons red wine vinegar

½ teaspoon salt (optional)

¼ teaspoon pepper

DIRECTION

» Heat oil in a saucepan over medium heat. Sauté celery, onions, carrots, shallots and garlic until onions are translucent. Add vegetable stock and lentils. Cook uncovered until lentils are just tender but not too soft. Before serving, add mustard, vinegar, salt and pepper.

Buon Appetito!

Pasta Fagioli

PREPARATION 10 Minutes   **TOTAL** 30 Minutes   **YIELD** 6

INGREDIENTS

2 teaspoons olive oil

1 small onion, chopped

2 cloves garlic, minced

2 cans (14 ½ oz each) fat-free, reduced sodium chicken broth

1 can diced tomatoes

1 can (15 oz) cannellini or white beans, rinsed and drained

½ cup ditalini or other small pasta

½ cup Swiss chard leaves or spinach leaves, coarsely chopped

¼ teaspoon salt

Parmesan cheese

DIRECTION

» Warm the oil in a large saucepan over medium heat. Add the onion and garlic. Cook, stirring occasionally for 3-5 minutes, or until onion is soft. Add the broth, tomatoes (with juice), beans and pasta. Cook, stirring occasionally, for 15 minutes. Add the Swiss chard and salt. Cook, stirring occasionally, for 2 to 3 minutes longer, or until Swiss chard is wilted. For added flavor, sprinkle grated cheese and black pepper on the pasta e fagioli just before serving.

Buon Appetito!

Tuscan Tomato Soup

PREPARATION 15 Minutes **TOTAL** 45 Minutes **YIELD** 6-8

INGREDIENTS

- 3lb ripe tomatoes
- 4 cups chicken stock
- 2 tablespoons extra virgin olive oil
- 1 large yellow onion
- 3 cloves garlic
- ½ cup basil
- ½ cup parmesan cheese

DIRECTION

» Grab a large pot, over medium heat add olive oil. Add the onion and saute, stir frequently until softened, about 5-7 minutes. Add the garlic and cook until softened. Add in the tomatoes and the stock, raise heat to high and bring to a boil. Reduce the heat to medium-low and cover, cook until tomatoes are softened about 30 minutes. Remove from heat and using a blender, puree the soup. Return soup to the pot and season with basil, salt and pepper. Serve with parmesan cheese on top

Buon Appetito!

The Sauce!
(fresh Tomato Sauce)

PREPARATION 15 Minutes **TOTAL** 45 Minutes **YIELD** 3.5 cups

INGREDIENTS

- 6 medium roma tomatoes
- ¼ cup chopped onion
- ½ cup chopped carrot
- 2 tablespoons tomato paste
- 1 garlic clove
- ½ teaspoon dried basil
- ½ teaspoon dried oregano
- ½ teaspoon fresh lemon juice
- ½ teaspoon brown sugar
- ¼ teaspoon salt

DIRECTION

» Place all ingredients into a vitamix or blender. Start blender on low and slowly increase. Blend for 1 minute until your hearts desired consistency. Pour into a saucepan and allow to simmer for 30 minutes over medium heat. Season with some salt and pepper to taste!

Buon Appetito!

Butternut Squash and Apple Soup

PREPARATION 15 Minutes **TOTAL** 45 Minutes **YIELD** 6-8

INGREDIENTS

2 tablespoons unsalted butter

2 tablespoons extra virgin olive oil

3 cups yellow onions (chopped)

2 large butternut squash (Diced)

4 apples (chopped)

2 tablespoons mild curry powder

2 cups apple juice or cider

DIRECTION

» Grab a large pot and warm the butter and olive oil over low heat. Add the onions and curry powder and allow to saute. Peel the squash and core the apples. Cut both into chunks. Add 2 cups of water to the pot, squash and apples and bring to a boil. Once boiling lower the heat back to low and cover, allow to cook for 30-40 minutes. Transfer the soup into a blender and blend it on up! Once the soup is pureed add back to the pot. Add in the 2 cups of apple juice or cider. Season with salt and pepper.

Buon Appetito!

Minestrone Soup

PREPARATION **15 Minutes** TOTAL **1 hour 30 Minutes** YIELD **6**

INGREDIENTS

4 tablespoons margarine (or butter)

3/4 cup chopped onion

1/4 cup chopped celery

1/2 cup chopped carrots

1 (19 ounce) can cannelloni beans

1/2 cup shredded cabbage

1 (14.5 ounce) can stewed tomatoes

1 tablespoon tomato paste

1 1/2 cups cubed potatoes

1-quart chicken broth

2 cloves garlic, minced

2 tablespoons dried parsley

1 teaspoon salt

1/2 cup shell macaroni

1/2 cup grated parmesan cheese

DIRECTION

» Melt butter or margarine in a heavy pot over medium heat. Add onion, celery and carrots; sauté for a few minutes. Add beans, cabbage, tomatoes, tomato paste, potatoes, stock, garlic, parsley and salt to the pot. Bring to a boil, cover and reduce heat. Simmer for approximately 1 hour until vegetables are barely tender. Add pasta and simmer for 30 minutes more. Serve with grated cheese.

Buon Appetito!

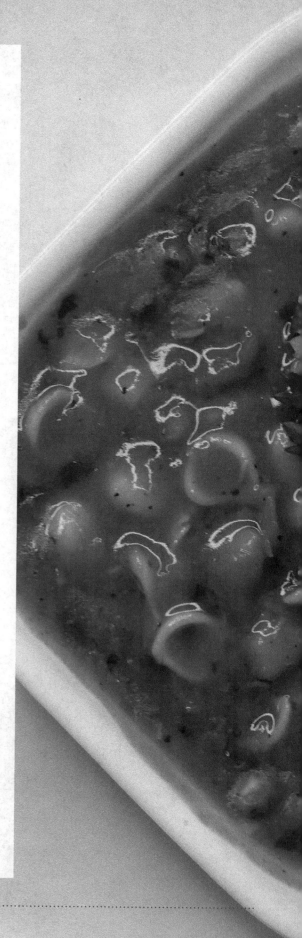

Sweet Potato Soup

PREPARATION 10 Minutes | TOTAL 40 Minutes | YIELD 6-8

INGREDIENTS

4 sweet potatoes (sliced)

1 yellow onion

3 cups chicken or vegetable stock

2 tablespoons butter

½ cup celery (diced)

3 garlic cloves

1 teaspoon dried oregano

¾ teaspoon ground ginger

½ teaspoon ground cumin

14 ounces coconut milk

DIRECTION

» Preheat the oven to 400ºF Line a baking sheet with parchment paper. Peel your sweet potatoes then cut into halves and coat with olive oil. Roast potatoes for 30. Transfer potatoes into a bowl and thoroughly mash. Grab a large saucepan, over medium heat add butter and allow to melt. Add in diced onion, celery and garlic and saute for 5 minutes. Sprinkle in oregano, ginger, cumin, salt and pepper. Stir in stock and coconut milk. Lower the heat to a low simmer. Add in your mashed sweet potato and mix together with all ingredients. For a smoother consistency grab a standing blender and puree the soup. Top with chopped chives, salt and pepper.

Buon Appetito!

Gazpacho

PREPARATION 20 Minutes   TOTAL 20 Minutes   YIELD 4-6

INGREDIENTS

1 cucumber, halved and seeded, but not peeled

2 red bell peppers, cored and seeded

4 plum tomatoes

1 red onion

3 garlic cloves, minced

23 oz tomato juice (3 cups)

¼ cup white wine vinegar

¼ cup extra-virgin olive oil

½ tablespoon kosher salt

1 teaspoon freshly ground black pepper

DIRECTION

» Roughly chop the cucumbers, bell peppers, tomatoes, and red onions into 1-inch cubes. Put each vegetable separately into a food processor fitted with a steel blade and pulse until it is coarsely chopped. Do not over process! After each vegetable is processed, combine them in a large bowl and add the garlic, tomato juice, vinegar, olive oil, salt, and pepper. Mix well and chill before serving. The longer gazpacho sits, the more the flavors develop. Overnight is best!

Buon Appetito!

breakfast

Flower Power Sunny-Side Eggs

PREPARATION 10 Minutes TOTAL 20 Minutes YIELD 2

INGREDIENTS

1 large bell pepper

1 tablespoon vegetable oil

4 large eggs

Chopped parsley for garnish

DIRECTION

» Slice bell pepper (or 4 in different colors) horizontally to make four ½ inch-thick rings and remove inner white flesh and seeds. In 12-inch nonstick skillet, heat vegetable oil on medium. Cook peppers 2 minutes. Turn peppers over; crack 1 egg into center of each ring. Cook, covered, until eggs reach desired doneness. Season with ¼ teaspoon salt and pepper. To serve, garnish with chopped parsley.

Buon Appetito!

Avocado Toast and Egg

PREPARATION 5 Minutes   TOTAL 10 Minutes   YIELD 1

INGREDIENTS

2 eggs

2 slices of multi-grain or whole grain bread (toasted)

1 small avocado

1 teaspoon lime juice

Sea salt and black pepper (to taste)

Parsley (optional for topping)

DIRECTION

» Prepare toast and fried eggs to personal preference. Peel and mash avocado with the lime juice, salt and pepper. Spread avocado evenly on each slice of toast then top each with a fried egg and any additional seasonings you prefer. Serve immediately.

Buon Appetito!

Egg and Cheese Sandwich

PREPARATION 10 Minutes   TOTAL 10 Minutes   YIELD 4

INGREDIENTS

4 large eggs

Kosher salt and pepper

1 tablespoon olive oil

2 oz. extra sharp cheddar cheese, coarsely grated

4 English muffins, toasted

2 cups baby spinach

4 thin slices ham (optional)

DIRECTION

» In a bowl, beat eggs with 1 tablespoon water and ¼ teaspoon salt and pepper. Heat oil in a large non stick skillet on medium heat. Add eggs and cook, stirring with a rubber spatula every few seconds, to desired doneness – 2 to 3 minutes for medium soft eggs. Spoon onto bottom half of each muffin and top with cheese, spinach and ham (if using). Sandwich with remaining top.

Buon Appetito!

Scrambled Egg Tacos

PREPARATION **10 Minutes** TOTAL **20 Minutes** YIELD **4**

INGREDIENTS

2 tablespoon olive oil

1 (15-oz can black beans, rinsed)

½ teaspoon cumin seeds

1 clove garlic, finely chopped

Kosher salt

Pepper

4 cups baby spinach

1 tablespoon fresh lemon juice

8 large eggs

8 yellow corn tortillas

Sour cream, crumbled queso fresco, and cilantro for serving

DIRECTION

» Heat 1 tablespoon oil in a large skillet on medium. Add beans, cumin, and garlic. Season with 1/8 teaspoon each salt and pepper and cook until garlic starts to turn golden brown, about 2 minutes. Add spinach, remove from heat, and toss together until leaves just barely wilt. Stir in lemon juice. In a large bowl, whisk together eggs, 1 tablespoon water, and 1/2 teaspoon each salt and pepper. Heat remaining tablespoon oil in a 10-inch nonstick skillet on medium. Add eggs and cook, stirring with a rubber spatula every few seconds to desired doneness, 2 to 3 minutes for medium-soft eggs. Lightly char tortillas under broiler or over a gas flame. Fill tortillas with beans, eggs, sour cream, queso fresco, and cilantro, if desired.

Buon Appetito!

Spinich and Prosciutto Frittata Muffins

PREPARATION **20 Minutes**   TOTAL **50 Minutes**   YIELD **6**

INGREDIENTS

6 large eggs

½ cup milk

¾ cup softened goat cheese, crumbled

5 oz baby spinach (wilted and chopped)

½ cup roasted red pepper, diced

2 oz prosciutto, sliced into ribbons

DIRECTION

» In a bowl, beat eggs with 1 tablespoon water and ¼ teaspoon salt and pepper. Heat oil in a large non stick skillet on medium heat. Add eggs and cook, stirring with a rubber spatula every few seconds, to desired doneness – 2 to 3 minutes for medium soft eggs. Spoon onto bottom half of each muffin and toppings with cheese, spinach and ham (if using). Sandwich with remaining toppings.

Buon Appetito!

Healthy Banana Bread

PREPARATION
10 Minutes

TOTAL
55 Minutes

YIELD:
8

INGREDIENTS

2 very ripe bananas, mashed (1 cup)

½ cup coconut sugar, or regular sugar

¾ cup almond milk, or any milk

1/3 cup extra-virgin olive oil, more for brushing

1 teaspoon vanilla extract

1 teaspoon apple cider vinegar

1 ½ cups whole wheat pastry flour (I recommend Bob's Red Mill)

½ cup almond flour

2 teaspoons baking powder

¼ teaspoon baking soda

1/2 teaspoon sea salt

½ teaspoon cinnamon

¼ teaspoon nutmeg

½ cup chopped walnuts

Topping 2 tablespoons chopped walnuts

1/1/2 tablespoon rolled oats

DIRECTION

» Preheat the oven to 350°F and brush a 9x5-inch loaf pan with a bit of olive oil. In a large bowl, combine the mashed bananas with the sugar, almond milk, olive oil, vanilla, and apple cider vinegar and whisk until combined. In a medium bowl combine the flours, baking powder, baking soda, salt, cinnamon, and nutmeg. Add the dry ingredients to the bowl with the wet ingredients and stir until just combined, then fold in the walnuts. Pour into the prepared pan and sprinkle with the chopped walnuts and oats. Bake for 42 to 50 minutes, or until a toothpick inserted in the middle comes out clean.

Buon Appetito!

Healthy Egg Muffins

🍴 PREPARATION
10 Minutes   ⏱ TOTAL
35 Minutes   🍴 YIELD
12

INGREDIENTS

12 large eggs

¼ cup nonfat milk

1 cup chopped fresh spinach

¾ cup quartered cherry tomatoes

½ cup diced onions

Sliced avocado, for serving

Salsa, for serving

Crumbled cotija or feta cheese, for serving

DIRECTION

» Preheat the oven to 350°F. Grease a muffin pan with cooking spray. In a large bowl, whisk together the eggs, nonfat milk and 1/2 teaspoon pepper. Stir in the spinach, tomatoes and onions. Divide the mixture evenly between the 12 muffin pan cups and bake the muffins for 20 to 25 minutes, or until the egg is fully cooked. Remove the muffins from the oven and let them cool for 5 minutes in the pan then use a knife to loosen the muffins from the cups. Top each muffin with sliced avocado, a dollop of salsa and a sprinkling of cheese then serve.
Buon Appetito!

Mexican Eggs

 PREPARATION
5 Minutes TOTAL **15 Minutes** YIELD **2**

INGREDIENTS

1-2 fresh mixed-color chilies

4 large eggs

1 (15 oz) can black beans

1 ripe avocado

1 lime

DIRECTION

» Finely slice the chilies (up to you how much!) Sprinkle half of them into a 12-inch non-stick frying pan on medium heat with 1 teaspoon of olive oil. One they start to sizzle, crack In the eggs, then spoon the black beans and half of the liquid from the can in and around the eggs. Season with sea salt and black pepper, cover and cook the eggs to your desired doneness. While the eggs are cooking, peel, pit the avocado and slice into thin wedges and dress with the lime juice.

Buon Appetito!

Scrambled Egg Omelet

 PREPARATION
5 Minutes TOTAL **15 Minutes** YIELD **1**

INGREDIENTS

4 eggs

12 ounces mixed color tomatoes (sliced)

1 fresh red chili

½ cup of fresh basil

5 ounces goat cheese

DIRECTION

» Slice the tomatoes and arrange around a platter. Dress with extra virgin olive oil, balsamic vinegar, salt and pepper. In a blender add your basil, salt, pepper, olive oil and ¼ cup water. Finely slice your red chili and the goat cheese. Grab a non stick frying pan and heat ½ tablespoon of olive oil. Beat the 4 eggs in a small bowl and pour into the pan. With a rubber spatula move the eggs gently around the pan. While the eggs are lightly scrambled add your goat cheese in the center and drizzle your basil sauce on top. This is where the magic happens, use the spatula to flip over the scramble. Flip one side then the other. Turn it upside down on top of your tomato platter. Top with salt, pepper, chilis and basil.

Buon Appetito!

Breakfast Yogurt Bark

PREPARATION
5 Minutes

YIELD
1 serving

INGREDIENTS

2 Cups Vanilla Greek Yogurt
1 cup blueberries
1 cup strawberries (sliced)

DIRECTION

» Grab a baking sheet and line with
parchment paper. Add your Greek yogurt
and smooth across the sheet. Arrange your
blueberries and strawberries on top and
place in the freezer for 30 minutes!
Break it into small pieces.

Buon Appetito!

Blueberry Almond Overnight Oats

PREPARATION
5 Minutes (must sit overnight)

YIELD
1 serving

INGREDIENTS

1/3 cup oats (gluten free or regular)

½ cup almond milk

1 teaspoon chia seeds

½ tablespoon maple syrup

1 teaspoon vanilla extract

2 tablespoons slivered almond

½ medium banana, sliced

1/3 cup blueberries

DIRECTION

» In an airtight container, mix oats, almond milk, chia seeds, maple syrup and vanilla. Seal the container and place in the fridge overnight. In the morning, stir oats and top with slivered almonds, sliced banana and blueberries.

Buon Appetito!

Banana Pancakes With Blueberry Sauce

PREPARATION **10 Minutes** TOTAL **20 Minutes** YIELD **6**

INGREDIENTS

- 1 banana
- 2 ½ cups whole wheat flour
- 2 tablespoons brown sugar
- 2 cups almond milk
- 1 teaspoon vanilla

Sauce

- 2 cups blueberries
- 2 tablespoons brown sugar
- 1 tablespoons lemon juice
- 1 tablespoons water
- 1 teaspoon vanilla extract

DIRECTION

» In a large mixing bowl mix banana, whole wheat flour, brown sugar, almond milk, vanilla and a dash of salt. Grab a non-stick cooking pan and heat over medium heat. Spray with a non-stick cook oil (coconut oil spray), add your pancake batter and cook until golden brown on both sides. In a small sauce pan, add your blueberries, brown sugar, lemon juice, vanilla and water. Allow to cook over medium heat and melt down blueberries until it becomes a thick sauce. Stir and mash down occasionally, should take 5-7 minutes. Pour Blueberry sauce over pancakes.

Buon Appetito!

lunch

Asian-style Cauliflower Tacos With Peanuts

PREPARATION **20 Minutes** TOTAL **25 Minutes** YIELD **8**

INGREDIENTS

1 head cauliflower	2 teaspoons cornstarch
1-inch fresh ginger (chopped)	2 teaspoons sriracha sauce
4 garlic cloves (minced)	1 large head iceberg lettuce
¼ cup unsalted peanuts	½ cup plain Greek yogurt
¼ cup soy sauce	1 cup shredded carrots
1 tablespoon brown sugar	½ cup green onions (sliced)

DIRECTION

» Preheat oven to 450°F Coat a baking sheet with non-stick spray. Chop the cauliflowers into bite size pieces. Arrange the cauliflower on the baking sheet and coat with cooking spray. Bake for 15 minutes or until lightly browned. Peel ginger then chop ginger, garlic and peanuts. In a small saucepan combine ginger, garlic, soy sauce, ¼ cup water, brown sugar, cornstarch and 1 teaspoon sriracha. Whisk it on up! Bring the mixture to a boil then reduce the heat to low to allow it to thicken. Once thickened remove from heat. Separate the leaves from the iceburge lettuce head and rinse. In a small bowl combine the yogurt, 2 tablespoons of water and 1 teaspoon sriracha. In a large bowl add the cauliflower then add the soy sauce mixture on top and toss. Fill each lettuce leaf with as much cauliflower as you desire. Top each taco with the yogurt sauce, green onion, carrot and peanuts.

Buon Appetito!

Crispy Garlic Chicken

PREPARATION 10 Minutes **TOTAL** 20 Minutes **YIELD** 2

INGREDIENTS

2 - 4 oz. skinless,
boneless chicken breasts

2 thick slices of
seeded whole-wheat bread

1 clove garlic

1 lemon

1 ¾ oz arugula

DIRECTION

» Place the chicken breasts between 2 sheets
of parchment paper, and pound to tenderize
and flatten to ½ inch thick. Tear the bread into a
food processor, peel, chop and add the garlic to
process into bread crumbs. Pour the crumbs over
the chicken. In a skillet, heat 1 tablespoon of olive
oil and cook each side of the chicken until crisp
and cooked through. Slice chicken into strips and
serve with arugula with juice of the lemon.

Buon Appetito!

Hearty Turkey Burgers

PREPARATION 10 Minutes   **TOTAL** 30 Minutes   **YIELD** 9

INGREDIENTS

2 tablespoons olive oil

3 medium yellow onions cut into ¼" pieces

1 clove garlic, finely chopped

1 ½ pound ground turkey

3 tablespoons dried bread crumbs

2 tablespoons barbecue sauce

3 tablespoons quick-cooking oatmeal

1 teaspoon dried basil

1 teaspoon dried oregano

1 tablespoon toasted wheat germ

¼ teaspoon salt

Ground black pepper

DIRECTION

» Warm the oil in the skillet over medium heat. Add the onions and garlic, cook over medium heat, stirring often, for about 10 minutes, or until onions start to brown. Add water, 1 tablespoon at a time, as necessary to prevent burning. Transfer them to a large bowl, and let them cool for about 10 minutes. Add in the turkey, bread crumbs, barbecue sauce, oatmeal, basil, oregano, wheat germ, salt and pepper to taste. Mix well. Shape the mixture into 9 burgers. Preheat grill to medium heat and refrigerate turkey burger patties until the grill is hot. Grill turkey burgers until patty appears to be cooked about half way up the side and then flip, grilling each side for about 4 to 5 minutes. Burger is done when surface is cracked and juices start to rise to the top.

Buon Appetito!

Grilled Cauliflower Steaks

PREPARATION 25 Minutes **TOTAL** 30 Minutes **YIELD** 4

INGREDIENTS

1 (12-oz.) jar roasted red peppers, drained

¼ cup almond butter

2 ½ tablespoons sherry vinegar

7 tablespoons olive oil, divided

1 ½ teaspoon kosher salt, divided

1 large head cauliflower

½ teaspoon freshly ground black pepper

1 (15.5-oz.) can chickpeas, drained and rinsed

4 cups baby arugula

3 radishes, thinly sliced

1 tablespoon fresh lemon juice (1 lemon)

2 oz. Manchego cheese, shaved (about 1 ¼ cups)

1/3 cup chopped roasted almonds

DIRECTION

» Process red peppers, almond butter, vinegar, 4 tablespoons oil, and ½ teaspoon salt in a blender, scraping down sides as needed, until smooth, about 1 minute. Preheat grill to medium-high 400°F– 450°F Cut cauliflower lengthwise into 4 "steaks" (3/4-inch-thick), leaving stem intact. Brush cauliflower with 2 tablespoons oil; season with black pepper and remaining 1 teaspoon salt. Grill cauliflower, turning occasionally, until stem is tender when pierced with a knife, 12 to 14 minutes. Meanwhile, add chickpeas, arugula, radishes, lemon juice, and remaining 1 tablespoon oil in a bowl. Divide red pepper sauce among plates. Top with cauliflower steaks, salad, cheese, and almonds.

Buon Appetito!

3 Pepper Chicken Basil Bowl

PREPARATION
10 Minutes

TOTAL
20 Minutes

YIELD
8

INGREDIENTS

2 teaspoon extra-virgin olive oil

1 ½ pounds boneless, skinless chicken thighs, cut into 1-inch pieces

1 medium yellow onion, chopped

1 medium orange, yellow and green bell peppers, chopped

1 jalapeno chili, seeded and finely chopped

2 garlic cloves, minced

1 large tomato, chopped

1 ¼ teaspoon sea salt

½ cup chopped fresh basil

4 cups cooked brown rice

DIRECTION

» Heat oil in a large skillet over high. Add chicken; cook, without stirring, until browned, about 3 minutes. Turn chicken; cook, stirring occasionally, until browned on all sides, about 6 to 7 minutes. Add onion, bell peppers, jalapeno and garlic; cook, stirring often, until vegetables are softened, about 8 minutes. Add tomato and salt; reduce heat to medium, and cook until tomato's release juices and vegetables and chicken are coated, 5 to 7 minutes. Remove from heat, stir in basil, serve over brown rice.

Buon Appetito!

Lemon Pepper Fish Tacos

PREPARATION 10 Minutes **TOTAL** 20 Minutes **YIELD** 8

INGREDIENTS

- 2 tablespoons extra-virgin olive oil
- 1 teaspoon freshly ground black pepper
- 1 teaspoon paprika
- ½ teaspoon salt
- 1 tablespoon lemon
- ½ pound Mahi Mahi (or other firm white fish)
- 3 cups slaw mix
- ½ cup cilantro leaves
- 8 hard corn taco shells, warmed
- Pico de gallo (optional)
- Guacamole (optional)
- Sour cream (optional)

DIRECTION

» Preheat oven to 325°F Heat taco shells in oven until crisp, 5 minutes. Season mahi mahi with 1 teaspoon ground black pepper, paprika, and 1/2 teaspoon salt. Heat olive oil in a skillet over medium-high heat. Cook mahi mahi in olive oil until fish flakes easily, about 3 minutes per side. Remove from skillet. Stir coleslaw and cilantro into skillet until coated and heated through. Break fish into bite size pieces. Fill each taco shell with coleslaw mixture, fish and additional toppings.

Buon Appetito!

Hummus and Veggie Sandwich

PREPARATION
10 Minutes

TOTAL
20 Minutes

YIELD
4

INGREDIENTS

1 ½ cloves garlic, peeled

1 (15 oz.) can garbanzo beans, drained

2 tablespoons olive oil

½ cup tahini

1 ½ lemons, juiced

1 pinch salt to taste

2 multi-grain bagels or ciabatta bread

1 cucumber, sliced

1 small red onion, sliced

Alfalfa or bean sprouts

DIRECTION

» Place garlic in a food processor and chop thoroughly. Add garbanzo beans and blend into a paste. Pour in 1 cup olive oil, tahini, lemon juice, and salt. Blend until smooth and creamy. Place hummus in a bowl. Build your sandwich by layering the hummus on your choice of bread, and topping with the cucumber, red onion and sprouts.

Buon Appetito!

Zucchini and Mozzarella Frittata

PREPARATION
15 Minutes

TOTAL
30 Minutes

YIELD
4

INGREDIENTS

4 tablespoons olive oil, divided

1 large zucchini, thinly sliced

1 tablespoon chopped fresh oregano leaves

4 cloves garlic, finely chopped

8 large eggs

1 cup mozzarella cheese

1 yellow onion

1/4 teaspoon red pepper flakes

1 teaspoon kosher salt

DIRECTION

» Preheat oven to 350°F. Heat 2 tablespoons oil in a 10-inch ovenproof skillet over medium heat. Add zucchini, onion, oregano, and garlic and cook, stirring often, until vegetables are slightly softened, 8 to 10 minutes. Whisk eggs, salt, and crushed red pepper until combined. Add remaining 2 tablespoons oil to skillet, tilting to distribute. Pour egg mixture over vegetables and shake skillet to help eggs settle. Cook over medium until edges begin to set, 2 to 3 minutes. Top with cheese. Transfer skillet to oven and cook until top is just set, 13 to 15 minutes. Let cool slightly. Gently slide frittata out of skillet and season with more crushed red pepper. Serve with salad.

Buon Appetito!

Indian Shrimp Curry

PREPARATION 15 Minutes   **TOTAL** 30 Minutes   **YIELD** 4

INGREDIENTS

- 2 tablespoons peanut oil
- ½ sweet onion, minced
- 2 cloves garlic, chopped
- 1 teaspoon ground ginger
- 1 teaspoon ground cumin
- 1 ½ teaspoons ground turmeric
- 1 teaspoon paprika
- ½ teaspoon red chili powder
- 1 (14.5 oz) can chopped tomatoes
- 1 (14 oz) can coconut milk
- 1 teaspoon salt
- 1 pound cooked, peeled and deveined shrimp
- 2 tablespoons chopped cilantro

DIRECTION

» Heat the oil in a large skillet over medium heat; cook the onion in the hot oil until translucent, about 5 minutes. Remove the skillet from the heat and allow it to cool slightly, about 2 minutes. Add the garlic, ginger, cumin, turmeric, paprika and ground chili to the onion and stir over low heat. Pour the tomatoes and coconut milk into the skillet; season with salt. Cook the mixture at a simmer, stirring occasionally, about 10 minutes. Stir the shrimp and cilantro into the sauce mixture and cook another minute before serving with rice.

Buon Appetito!

Meatball Buns

PREPARATION 10 Minutes **TOTAL** 20 Minutes **YIELD** 4

INGREDIENTS

1 lb lean ground turkey

8 teaspoons basil pesto

1 can plum tomatoes

1 ball goat cheese

4 soft pretzel buns

DIRECTION

» In a large bowl scrunch the ground turkey with 4 teaspoons of the pesto, salt and pepper. Roll the turkey into 12 individual balls. Brown the meatballs over a non-stick frying pan on high heat with 1 tablespoon of olive oil. Pour in the tomatoes and a ¼ cup of water once the meatballs are golden brown and break them up with a wooden spoon. Bring to a boil, slice the goat cheese and lay over the meatballs, allow to thicken for 5 minutes. Toast your buns, split them and spread a teaspoon of basil pesto sauce on each side. Lay the meatballs and goat cheese with a little sauce on top of each bun. Sandwich together.

Buon Appetito!

Pan Seared Red Snapper

PREPARATION 10 Minutes **TOTAL** 20 Minutes **YIELD** 2

INGREDIENTS

2 (4 oz) red snapper fillets

1 tablespoon olive oil

1 lemon, juiced

2 tablespoons rice wine vinegar

1 teaspoon Dijon mustard

1 tablespoon honey

¼ chopped green onions

1 teaspoon ground ginger

DIRECTION

» Rinse snapper under cold water, and pat dry. In a shallow bowl, mix together olive oil, lemon, rice vinegar, mustard, honey, green onions and ginger. Heat a non-stick skillet over medium heat. Dip snapper fillets in marinade to coat both sides and place in skillet. Cook for 2 to 3 minutes on each side. Pour remaining marinade into skillet. Reduce heat and simmer for 2 to 3 minutes, or until fish flakes easily with a fork.

Buon Appetito!

Homemade Pizza

PREPARATION **10 Minutes**   TOTAL **20 Minutes**   YIELD **3-4**

INGREDIENTS

Dough

2 cups all-purpose flour

2 teaspoons baking powder

½ teaspoon baking soda

1 cup Greek yogurt

2 tablespoons olive oil

1 cup water

Toppings

Basil

Cherry tomatoes

Red onion

Oregano

Mozzarella cheese

Balsamic glaze

DIRECTION

» Preheat Oven to 400ºF In a large mixing bowl add, flour, baking powder, baking soda, Greek yogurt, olive oil and water. With your hands turn the dough onto a lightly floured surface and gently knead into a smooth ball. Stretch the dough to fit a pizza pan. In a non-stick skillet add some olive oil and place the dough inside, cooking until golden brown on each side. Once done place on a pizza tray or cooking sheet and allow to cool. In a large bowl add cherry tomatoes, red onion, oregano, salt and pepper and mix it on up. Add the tomato mixture on top of the dough and bake in the oven for 15 minutes. Once done, allow the pizza to cool, add basil and balsamic glaze.

Buon Appetito!

Sesame Noodle Bowl

PREPARATION **10 Minutes**   TOTAL **15 Minutes**   YIELD **4**

INGREDIENTS

Sesame Sauce
¼ cup tahini
¼ cup warm water
3 tablespoons light soy sauce
1 tablespoon sesame oil
1 tablespoon rice vinegar
1 garlic clove

Bowl
1 pack Chinese egg noodles or linguine
2 cucumbers (diced)
1 lb chicken breast
1 cup pineapple (diced)
Sesame seeds
2 tablespoons olive oil

DIRECTION

» In a small bowl whisk together the sesame sauce, tahini, water, soy sauce, oil, vinegar and garlic. Grab a sauce pan and bring water to boil, cook noodles thoroughly. Grab your chicken, season with salt and pepper. In a large non-stick pan, over medium heat, add olive oil and cook chicken thoroughly. In a large bowl add your noodles, divide the pineapple, cucumber, chicken. Add your sesame sauce mixture on top of the noodles and top with sesame seeds.

Buon Appetito!

Eggplant With Feta Cheese and Yogurt Sauce

PREPARATION 20 Minutes   **TOTAL** 30 Minutes   **YIELD** 5

INGREDIENTS

1 tablespoon lemon juice

1 tablespoon olive or vegetable oil

1 (1 -1/2 pound) eggplant, cut into ¾-inch slices

Sauce

¾ cup low fat plain yogurt

1/3 cup crumbled feta cheese

¼ cup chopped red onion

3 tablespoons chopped fresh mint leaves

1 tablespoon lemon juice

1 teaspoon finely chopped garlic

1/8 teaspoon red pepper flakes

DIRECTION

» Heat broiler. Stir together lemon juice and oil; brush both sides of eggplant. Place eggplant slices on baking sheet. Broil 6 to 8 inches from heat, turning once, until tender and lightly browned (6 to 8 minutes).

» Meanwhile, in small bowl combine all sauce ingredients; mix well. Serve over warm eggplant slices.

Buon Appetito!

Apple, Walnut and Brie Salad

PREPARATION 10 Minutes **TOTAL** 10 Minutes **YIELD** 4

INGREDIENTS

2 red apples, cored and thinly sliced

3 cups spring mixed salad greens

½ cup Brie cheese

1/3 cup toasted walnut pieces

Vinaigrette

½ cup olive oil

¼ cup balsamic vinegar

1 teaspoon honey

1 teaspoon Dijon mustard

1 shallot, minced

1 clove garlic, minced

Salt and ground black pepper
to taste

DIRECTION

» Combine the olive oil, balsamic vinegar, honey, Dijon mustard, shallot, garlic, salt, and black pepper together in a glass jar with a lid. Replace lid on the jar and shake vigorously until thoroughly combined. Toss the apple slices with the vinaigrette in a bowl until evenly coated; add the greens and toss again; top with the Brie and walnuts just before serving.

Buon Appetito!

Moroccan Turnip and Chickpea Braise

PREPARATION **15 Minutes**   TOTAL **45 Minutes**   YIELD **4**

INGREDIENTS

2 tablespoons olive oil

1 small onion, thinly sliced

2 carrots, halved lengthwise and cut crosswise into ½-inch thick moons

2 tablespoons tomato paste

1-pound turnips, peeled and cut into ¾-inch cubes

1 teaspoon kosher salt

½ teaspoon cumin

¼ teaspoon cayenne pepper

1 - 14-15 ounce can chickpeas, drained and rinsed

1 cup low sodium chicken or vegetable broth

½ teaspoon freshly ground black pepper

1/3 cup chopped cilantro

Cooked rice or couscous (optional)

DIRECTION

» In a large deep saucepan, heat oil over medium heat. Add onion and carrots and cook, stirring occasionally, for 5 minutes. Add tomato paste, turnips, salt, cumin and cayenne pepper and stir well. Add chickpeas and broth. Raise heat to medium-high and bring to a boil. Decrease heat to low, cover and simmer until vegetables are tender, 15 to 20 minutes. Stir in black pepper and cilantro. Serve over rice or couscous.

Buon Appetito!

Grilled Veggie Sandwich

PREPARATION 20 Minutes   **TOTAL** 40 Minutes   **YIELD** 4

INGREDIENTS

- ¼ cup mayonnaise
- 3 cloves garlic, minced
- 1 tablespoon lemon juice
- 1/8 cup olive oil
- 1 cup sliced red bell peppers
- 1 small zucchini, sliced
- 1 red onion, sliced
- 1 small yellow squash, sliced
- 2 (4"x6") focaccia bread pieces, split horizontally
- ½ cup crumbled feta cheese

DIRECTION

» In a bowl, mix the mayonnaise, minced garlic, and lemon juice. Set aside in the refrigerator. Preheat the grill for high heat. Brush vegetables with olive oil on each side. Brush grate with oil. Place bell peppers and zucchini closest to the middle of the grill, and set onion and squash pieces around them. Cook for about 3 minutes, turn, and cook for another 3 minutes. The peppers may take a bit longer. Remove from grill, and set aside. Spread some of the mayonnaise mixture on the cut sides of the bread, and sprinkle each one with feta cheese. Place on the grill cheese side up, and cover with lid for 2 to 3 minutes. This will warm the bread, and slightly melt the cheese. Watch carefully so the bottoms don't burn. Remove from grill, and layer with the vegetables. Serve as open faced grilled sandwiches.

Buon Appetito!

Tuna and Bean Salad

PREPARATION **10 Minutes**   TOTAL **20 Minutes**   YIELD **4**

INGREDIENTS

- 2 bunches watercress, tough ends trimmed
- ¼ cup water
- 1 clove garlic, thinly sliced
- 1 can (12 oz) tuna, packed in water, drained and flaked
- ½ cup canned cannellini beans, drained and rinsed
- ¼ sweet white onion, finely chopped
- ½ cup roasted red pepper, chopped
- 3 tablespoons mayonnaise
- 2 tablespoons fat-free sour cream
- 1 tablespoon red wine vinegar
- 1 ½ teaspoons capers, drained and rinsed
- Salt
- Black pepper

DIRECTION

» Coarsely chop the watercress stems until you have ½ cup. Rinse and dry the remaining watercress sprigs and set aside. In a small saucepan, combine the chopped stems, water, and garlic. Bring to a boil over medium-high heat. Reduce the heat to low. Cover and simmer until the stems are bright green, about 1 to 2 minutes. Drain and place in a large bowl. Add the tuna, beans, onion, and roasted pepper to the bowl and blend.
In a blender or food processor, combine the mayonnaise, sour cream, vinegar, capers, salt and black pepper to taste. Puree until smooth. Serve the tuna mixture on the reserved watercress sprigs and drizzle with the dressing.

Buon Appetito!

Balsamic Tomato and Mozzarella Salad

PREPARATION **20 Minutes**   TOTAL **35 Minutes**   YIELD **4**

INGREDIENTS

1 tablespoon balsamic vinegar

2 teaspoons extra-virgin olive oil

1 clove garlic, minced

¼ teaspoon salt

1/8 teaspoon ground black pepper

2 large red bell peppers,
halved and seeded

2 large tomatoes,
cut into ½"-thick slices

2 oz fresh mozzarella cheese,
cut into 4 slices

1/3 cup fresh basil leaves

DIRECTION

» Preheat the broiler. Coat a broiler-pan with cooking spray. In a cup, whisk together the vinegar, olive oil, garlic, salt and black pepper. Set aside. Place the bell peppers, skin side up, on the prepared pan. Broil, without turning, for 10 minutes, or until the skins are blackened and blistered in spots. Place the peppers in a paper bag and seal. Let stand for 10 minutes until cooled. Peel the skin from the peppers and discard. Cut the peppers into ½"-wide strips. Arrange tomato slices on a platter. Place the cheese slices over the tomatoes. Layer the pepper strips on top and sprinkle with julienned basil. Drizzle the dressing over the salad and let stand for 15 minutes to allow the flavors to blend.

Buon Appetito!

dinner

Turkey Veggie Meatloaf Cups

PREPARATION **20 Minutes**   TOTAL **50 Minutes**   YIELD **20**

INGREDIENTS

2 cups coarsely chopped zucchini

1 ½ cups coarsely chopped onions

1 red bell pepper (or carrots) coarsely chopped

1 pound extra lean ground turkey

½ cup uncooked couscous

1 egg

2 tablespoons Worcestershire sauce

1 tablespoon Dijon mustard

½ barbecue sauce, or as needed

DIRECTION

» Preheat oven to 400ºF and spray 20 muffin cups with cooking spray. Place zucchini, onions, and red bell pepper into a food processor and pulse several times until finely chopped but not liquefied. Place the vegetables into a bowl, and mix in ground turkey, couscous, egg, Worcestershire sauce, and Dijon mustard until thoroughly combined. Fill each prepared muffin cup about 3/3 full. Top each cup with about 1 teaspoon of barbecue sauce. Bake in the preheated oven until juices run clear, about 25 minutes. Internal temperature of a muffin by an instant-read meat thermometer should be at least 160ºF Let stand 5 minutes before serving.

Buon Appetito!

Chicken Kabobs With Yogurt Marinade

PREPARATION 15 Minutes TOTAL 60 Minutes YIELD 4

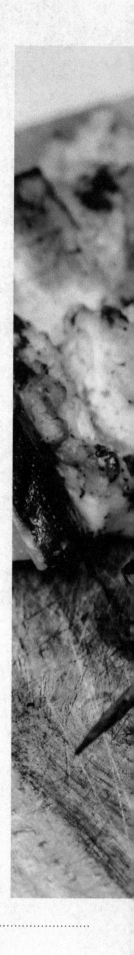

INGREDIENTS

3 skinless boneless chicken breast halves (about 6 oz)

1 cup low-fat plain yogurt

2 green onions, including tender green parts, chopped

1 clove garlic, crushed

½ teaspoon dried oregano

½ teaspoon cumin

Salt and freshly ground pepper

½ red bell pepper, seeded and cut into 8 equal pieces

½ yellow bell pepper, seeded and cut into 8 equal pieces

1 small zucchini, trimmed, halved lengthwise, and cut into 8 pieces

DIRECTION

» Cut the chicken into 1 ½ to 2-inch cubes and set aside. To make the marinade, combine the yogurt, green onions, garlic, oregano, cumin, ½ teaspoon salt, and ½ teaspoon pepper in a glass bowl. Add the cubed chicken and mix well. Cover and refrigerate for 1 hour. Preheat a gas grill on high heat, then reduce to medium. If using wooden skewers, soak 4 long skewers in water for 30 minutes. On each skewer, thread 4 pieces of the chicken and 2 pieces each of the red and yellow bell pepper, and the zucchini, alternating the chicken and vegetables. Coat kabobs with the remaining marinade. Cook over medium heat for 15 minutes total.

Buon Appetito!

Easy White Chili

PREPARATION 15 Minutes **TOTAL** 45 Minutes **YIELD** 8

INGREDIENTS

2 tablespoons olive oil

2 onions, chopped

4 cloves garlic, Minced

4 cooked, boneless chicken breast halves, chopped

3 (14.5oz) cans chicken broth

2 (4 oz) cans green chile peppers, chopped

2 teaspoons ground cumin

2 teaspoons dried oregano

1 ½ teaspoons cayenne pepper

5 (14.5 oz) cans great Northern beans, undrained

1 cup shredded Monterey Jack Cheese

DIRECTION

» Heat 1 teaspoon of the oil in a large pot over medium heat. Add the chicken and brown on all sides, remove and set aside. In the same pot, add the other teaspoon of olive oil, the onions and garlic and sauté for 10 minutes, or until onions are tender. Return the chicken to the pot, add the chicken broth, green chile peppers, cumin, oregano and cayenne pepper and bring to a boil. Reduce heat to low and add the beans. Simmer for 20 to 30 minutes, or until heated thoroughly. Pour into individual bowls and top with the cheese.

Buon Appetito!

Sicilian Swordfish

PREPARATION 10 Minutes   **TOTAL** 30 Minutes   **YIELD** 4

INGREDIENTS

4 swordfish steaks, about ½ lb each

1 tablespoon garlic powder

1 tablespoon basil

1 teaspoon fennel seeds, ground

¼ teaspoon red pepper flakes

Salt and freshly ground pepper

SALSA

¼ cup chopped, pitted Sicilian olives

1 cup chopped tomatoes

¼ cup chopped fresh basil

3 cloves garlic, minced

¼ teaspoon cayenne pepper

2 tablespoons extra-virgin olive oil, plus more for coating

Juice of ½ lemon

DIRECTION

» Preheat gas grill on high heat. Oil the grill rack and coat the fish with oil. To make the spice rub, mix together the garlic powder, basil, fennel seeds, red pepper flakes, 1 ½ teaspoon salt, and 1 teaspoon pepper in a small bowl. Sprinkle both sides of each swordfish generously with the spice rub. To make the salsa, mix together the olives, tomatoes, basil, garlic, cayenne, the 2-tablespoons oil, and the lemon juice in a bowl. Taste and season with salt. Set aside. Grill the swordfish directly over high heat, turning once, until grill-marked, firm to the touch, and opaque throughout, 3-4 minutes on each side. To serve, top with the salsa or serve with the salsa alongside.

Buon Appetito!

Greek Shrimp

PREPARATION 10 Minutes **TOTAL** 30 Minutes **YIELD** 4

INGREDIENTS

4 Tablespoons extra-virgin olive oil

2 shallots, mince

2 cloves garlic, minced

½ cup dry vermouth or dry white wine

6 plum (Roma) tomatoes, chopped, or 1 can (14.5 oz) tomatoes, drained and finely chopped, juice reserved

1 Tablespoon dried Greek oregano

Sea salt

Red pepper flakes

Sweet Hungarian paprika to taste

2/3 cup coarsely chopped feta cheese

2 lb. large shrimp, shelled with tail intact, deveined

2 tablespoon minced fresh mint, plus sprigs for garnish

DIRECTION

»   In a large saute pan over medium heat, heat the oil. Add the shallots and sauté until translucent, about 3 minutes. Add the garlic and sauté until fragrant, about 1 minute. Add the wine and tomatoes (but not their juice). Add the oregano and season to taste with salt, red pepper flakes, and paprika. Bring to a boil over high heat, then reduce to medium and cook, stirring often, until the tomatoes begin to soften, about 5 minutes. Add some of the reserved tomato juice if you prefer a thinner sauce. Stir in the cheese, then the shrimp. Cover the pan, reduce the heat to low, and cook until the shrimp are evenly pink and the cheese is beginning to melt, about 3 minutes. Sprinkle with the minced mint and garnish with the sprigs.

Buon Appetito!

Peachy Pork Chops

PREPARATION 10 Minutes **TOTAL** 30 Minutes **YIELD** 2

INGREDIENTS

- 2 pork chops (8 ounces)
- 4 garlic cloves
- 2 sprigs rosemary
- 1 can of peach halves (15 ounces)
- ¼ cup sherry cooking wine

DIRECTION

» Grab a non-stick frying pan, place on high heat with a ½ tablespoons of olive oil. Add your chops and cook on each side for 5 minutes or until lightly golden brown. While the chops cook, mince your garlic and strip the rosemary leaves from the sprigs. Removes the chops from the heat and leave them on a cutting board to cool. Sprinkle in your garlic and allow to saute until golden. Then add your rosemary and peaches. Then return the chop to the pan and add your sherry cooking wine. Carefully set fire and stand back. One the flames subside, plate your chops and top with salt, pepper and rosemary.

Buon Appetito!

Garlic Butter Filet

PREPARATION 10 Minutes **TOTAL** 30 Minutes **YIELD** 2

INGREDIENTS

- 2 filet mignon (6 ounces) (room temperature)
- 2 tablespoons extra-virgin olive oil
- 4 tablespoons butter
- 2 sprigs rosemary
- Kosher Salt & fresh ground pepper

DIRECTION

» Preheat oven to 400°F Grab a large skillet, add olive oil and heat on high heat. Season room temperature steaks with salt and pepper on both sides. Add steaks to skillet and cook until seared, about 5 minutes. Flip the steak and add butter and rosemary to the skillet. Baste the steaks with butter and rosemary and cook for another 5 minutes. Grab the skillet and toss it into the oven for about 5-10 minutes depending on your desired temperature. Remove the steaks from pan and allow to cool on a cutting board. Plate the steaks, add salt, pepper and rosemary.

Buon Appetito!

Easy Healthy
Baked Salmon

PREPARATION **10 Minutes**   TOTAL **30 Minutes**   YIELD **4**

INGREDIENTS

4 salmon fillets about 6 oz. each

2 tablespoons olive oil

½ teaspoon salt

¼ teaspoon black pepper

½ teaspoon orange peel

¼ teaspoon sugar (optional)

1 medium lemon

DIRECTION

» Preheat oven to 400°F and grease a large baking sheet. Arrange salmon on the baking sheet and squeeze ½ lemon juice over fillets. In a small bowl combine the salt, black pepper, orange peel and sugar. Spoon over salmon fillets being sure to rub all over top and sides so it has no dry spots. Drizzle the 2 tablespoons of olive oil over the salmon. Bake for 15-18 minutes until salmon is opaque and flaky when pulled apart with a fork. You can broil the last 1-2 minutes if desired.

Buon Appetito!

Orange Glaze
Rosemary Salmon

PREPARATION
10 Minutes
TOTAL
30 Minutes
YIELD
2

INGREDIENTS

4 skinless salmon fillets (6 ounces)

2 teaspoons olive oil

2 garlic cloves (minced)

2 ½ teaspoon rosemary (minced)

¼ cup chicken broth

1 ½ teaspoons orange zest

2/3 cup fresh orange juice

1 tablespoon lemon juice

1 ½ tablespoon honey

2 ½ teaspoons cornstarch

DIRECTION

» Grab a large non-stick skillet, add olive oil and heat over medium-high heat. Season salmon fillets with salt, pepper and cook until lightly browned on each side, about 4 minutes. Plate salmon and allow to cool. In the skillet add garlic and rosemary and allow to saute for 1 minute. Then add chicken broth and allow the sauce to simmer. Stir in orange zest, orange juice, lemon juice and honey and occasionally stir. Add cornstarch, salt and pepper and bring to a boil. Allow the sauce to boil for about 1 minute then remove from heat. Return your fillets to the pan and spoon the sauce over the salmon.

Buon Appetito!

Easy Chicken Francese

PREPARATION
8-10 Minutes   TOTAL 30 Minutes   YIELD 6

INGREDIENTS

- ½ cup almond flour
- 4 eggs (beaten)
- 1-pound skinless chicken cutlets
- ½ cup white cooking wine
- 2 cups chicken broth
- 1 teaspoon parsley
- ¼ cup butter
- 2 lemons (juiced)
- 1 teaspoon cornstarch

DIRECTION

» Preheat oven to 350°F In a medium bowl beat 4 eggs, coat chicken with egg and flour. In a medium saucepan add wine, broth, parsley, salt, pepper, butter and lemon juice. Stir occasionally while the sauce heats on medium to low heat. Then add cornstarch until sauce thickens. Grab a baking tin and arrange chicken, pour sauce on top and bake for 15 minutes.

Buon Appetito!

Momma's Chicken Traybake

PREPARATION 10 Minutes **TOTAL** 45 Minutes **YIELD** 6

INGREDIENTS

4 mixed color peppers, chopped

4-6 carrots, chopped

2 red onions, chopped

1 whole chicken, cut into 8 pieces

4 celery stalks, chopped

6 medium size potatoes
(Russet or Yukon Gold), cubed

2 thyme sprigs

2 tablespoons oregano

2 lemons (juiced)

½ cup red wine vinegar

Olive oil

Sea salt and freshly
ground black pepper

DIRECTION

» Preheat oven to 425°F Using a
large sharp knife cut chicken
into 8 pieces, salt and pepper
both sides, set aside. Chop all of
the vegetables and arrange in a
roasting pan. Add the chicken to
the pan, skin side up. Squeeze in
the juice of 2 lemons and ½ cup
red wine vinegar, and brush the
chicken with olive oil. Sprinkle the
oregano and thyme all over the
chicken and vegetables. Reduce
the oven temperature to 375°F and
roast it all for 50 minutes or until
thoroughly cooked.
Buon Appetito!

Chicken Thighs With Spinach and Shallots

PREPARATION 10 Minutes   **TOTAL** 45 Minutes   **YIELD** 6

INGREDIENTS

6 boneless skinless chicken thighs

½ teaspoon seasoned salt (season with your choice of dried herbs)

½ teaspoon pepper

1 ½ teaspoons olive oil

4 shallots, thinly sliced

1/3 cup cup white wine or reduced-sodium chicken broth

1 package (10 oz.) fresh spinach, trimmed

¼ teaspoon salt

¼ cup reduced-fat sour cream

DIRECTION

» Sprinkle the chicken with seasoned salt and pepper. In a large nonstick skillet, heat oil over medium heat. Add chicken; cook until a thermometer reads 170 F, about 6 minutes on each side. Remove from pan; keep warm. In same pan, cook and stir shallots until tender. Add wine; bring to a boil. Cook until wine is reduced by half. Add spinach and salt; cook and stir just until spinach is wilted. Stir in sour cream; serve with chicken.

Buon Appetito!

Ginger Veggie Stir Fry

PREPARATION **25 Minutes** TOTAL **40 Minutes** YIELD **4**

INGREDIENTS

- 1 tablespoon cornstarch
- 1 ½ cloves garlic, crushed
- 2 teaspoons chopped fresh ginger root, divided
- ¼ cup vegetable oil, divided
- 1 small head broccoli, cut into florets
- ½ cup snow peas
- ¾ cup carrots, julienned
- ½ cup halved green beans
- 2 tablespoons soy sauce
- 2 ½ tablespoons water
- ¼ cup chopped oion
- ½ tablespoon salt
- 1 cup Jasmine rice

DIRECTION

» In a large bowl, blend cornstarch, garlic, 1 teaspoon ginger, and 2 tablespoons vegetable oil until cornstarch is dissolved. Mix in broccoli, snow peas, carrots, and green beans, tossing to lightly coat. Heat remaining 2 tablespoons oil in a large skillet or wok over medium heat. Cook vegetables in oil for 2 minutes, stirring constantly to prevent burning. Stir in soy sauce and water. Mix in onion, salt, and remaining 1 teaspoon ginger. Cook until vegetables are tender but still crisp. Serve over a bed of steamed jasmine rice.

Buon Appetito!

Marrakesh Vegetable Curry

🍴 **PREPARATION** 15 Minutes   ⏱ **TOTAL** 50 Minutes   🍽 **YIELD** 4

INGREDIENTS

1 sweet potato, peeled and cubed

1 medium eggplant, cubed

1 green bell pepper, chopped

1 red bell pepper, chopped

2 carrots, chopped

1 onion, chopped

6 tablespoons olive oil

3 cloves garlic, minced

1 teaspoon ground turmeric

1 tablespoon curry powder

1 teaspoon ground cinnamon

¾ tablespoon sea salt

¾ teaspoon cayenne powder

1 (15 oz.) can
garbanzo beans, drained

¼ cup blanched almonds

1 zucchini, sliced

2 tablespoons raisins

1 cup orange juice

10 ounces spinach

DIRECTION

» In a large Dutch oven pot place sweet potato, eggplant, peppers, carrots, onion, and 3 tablespoons oil. Sauté over medium heat for 5 minutes. In a medium saucepan, place 3 tablespoons olive oil, garlic, turmeric, curry powder, cinnamon. Salt and pepper and sauté over medium heat for 3 minutes. Pour garlic and spice mixture into the Dutch oven with vegetables in it. Add the garbanzo beans, almonds, zucchini, raisins, and orange juice. Simmer 20 minutes, covered. Add spinach to pot and cook for 5 more minutes. Serve over your favorite rice!

Buon Appetito!

Vegetable Paella

PREPARATION **20 Minutes**   TOTAL **50 Minutes**   YIELD **8**

INGREDIENTS

- 2 tablespoons olive or vegetable oil
- 1 medium onion, chopped
- 1 medium red pepper, chopped
- 2 teaspoons finely chopped fresh garlic
- 1 cup uncooked long grain rice
- 1 (14.5 oz.) can stewed tomatoes
- 1 (14.5 oz.) can vegetable broth
- 2 medium carrots, finely chopped
- 1 teaspoon paprika
- 1 (6.5 oz.) jar marinated artichoke hearts, drained
- ½ small eggplant, cubed
- 1 small zucchini, cubed 1-inch
- ½ cup frozen peas
- ¼ cup chopped fresh parsley

DIRECTION

» In Dutch oven pot combine oil, onion, red pepper and garlic. Cook over medium high heat, stirring occasionally, until onion and pepper is softened (5 minutes). Add rice. Continue cooking 1 minute, stirring constantly, to coat with oil. Add tomatoes, broth, carrots and paprika. Bring to a boil. Cover; reduce heat to medium low. Cook 10 minutes, stirring once. Add artichoke hearts, eggplant and zucchini. Continue cooking, stirring once, until broth is almost absorbed (10 to 12 minutes). Add peas and parsley. Continue cooking until heated through (3 to 4 minutes).

Buon Appetito!

Bake Spaghetti Squash With Parmesan

PREPARATION 10 Minutes **TOTAL** 50 Minutes **YIELD** 2

INGREDIENTS

1 medium spaghetti squash

8 tablespoons (1 stick) butter

3 tablespoons mixed herbs such as parsley, chives and oregano, chopped

1 garlic clove, crushed

1 shallot, chopped

1 tablespoon lemon juice

½ cup parmesan cheese, finely grated

Salt and black pepper

DIRECTION

» Preheat the oven to 350ºF Cut the squash in half lengthwise. Place the halves, cut side down, in a roasting pan. Pour a little water around them, and then bake for 40 minutes until tender. Do not allow them to burn – cover with foil if needed. Meanwhile, put the butter, herbs, garlic,shallot and lemon juice in a food processor and process unti thoroughly blended and creamy in consistency. Season to taste. When the squash is tender, scrape out any seeds and cut a thin slice from the base of each half, so they will sit level. Place the squash halves on serving plates. Using a fork, pull out a few of the spaghetti-like strands in the center to make room for filling. Add a dollop of herb butter, then sprinkle with a little of the parmesan cheese. Can also be served with tomato sauce instead of pasta!

Buon Appetito!

Roast Pork Tenderloin

PREPARATION 10 Minutes   **TOTAL** 70 Minutes   **YIELD** 6

INGREDIENTS

1 (2-lb) boneless pork tenderloin

Kosher salt

2 lb. baby potatoes, quartered

½ plus tablespoon of extra-virgin olive oil, divided

¼ cup maple syrup

3 cloves garlic, minced

1 tablespoon whole grain mustard

2 teaspoon finely chopped rosemary

¼ teaspoon red pepper flakes

DIRECTION

» Preheat oven to 400°F Season tenderloin on both sides with salt and pepper. Place potatoes in a 9"x13" baking dish and drizzle with 2 tablespoons oil and season with salt and pepper. In a small bowl, whisk together remaining ½ cup oil, maple syrup, garlic, mustard, rosemary and red pepper flakes. Season with salt and pepper then brush over tenderloin. Roast for 1 hour or until potatoes are tender and tenderloin is cooked through. Internal temperature should read 145°F

Buon Appetito!

Classic
Stuffed
Peppers

PREPARATION 20 Minutes   TOTAL 80 Minutes   YIELD 6

INGREDIENTS

1 pound ground beef (or chicken, turkey or pork)

½ cup uncooked long grain white rice

1 cup water

6 green peppers

2 (8oz.) cans tomato sauce

1 tablespoon Worcestershire sauce

¼ teaspoon garlic powder

¼ teaspoon onion powder

¼ teaspoon salt and pepper to taste

1 teaspoon Italian seasoning

DIRECTION

» Preheat oven to 350°F Place the rice and water in a saucepan, and bring to a boil. Reduce heat, cover, and cook 20 minutes. In a skillet over medium heat, cook the beef until evenly browned. Remove and discard the tops, seeds and membranes of the bell peppers. Arrange them in a baking dish with the hollowed side facing up. (slice the bottoms of the peppers if necessary, so that they will stand upright). In a bowl, mix the browned beef, cooked rice, 1 can tomato sauce, Worcestershire sauce, garlic powder, onion powder, salt and pepper. Spoon an equal amount of the mixture into each hollowed pepper. Mix the remaining tomato sauce and Italian seasoning in a bowl, and pour over the stuffed peppers. Bake 1 hour in the preheated oven, basting with sauce every 15 minutes, until the peppers are tender.

Buon Appetito!

Game Day Chili

PREPARATION **20 Minutes**   TOTAL **30 Minutes**   YIELD **8**

INGREDIENTS

2 tablespoon olive oil

2 teaspoon garlic cloves, chopped

1 large onion, chopped

4 carrots, chopped

1 lb. lean ground beef

– ½ pound lean pork

2 (15-oz.) cans dark red kidney beans, drained and rinsed

2 (15-oz.) cans light red kidney beans, drained and rinsed

2 (15-oz) can tomato sauce

1 (10-oz.) can diced tomatoes and green chilies

2 tablespoons chili powder

1 tablespoon garlic powder

2 teaspoons kosher salt

1 teaspoon ground cumin

½ teaspoon black pepper

Creole seasoning (to taste)

Shredded Cheddar cheese

DIRECTION

» Heat oil in a large pot over medium heat. Add chopped garlic; cook, stirring constantly, until fragrant about 1 minute. Add carrots and onion; cook, stirring often, until softened, about 6 minutes. Add ground beef and pork; cook stirring often until cooked through, about 10 minutes. Add beans, tomato sauce, diced tomatoes, and green chilis; cook, stirring often about 5 minutes. Stir in chili powder, garlic powder, salt, cumin, pepper, and creole seasoning. Cover and reduce heat to low until ready to serve. Top with cheese and diced onions.

Buon Appetito!

Easy Garlic Lemon Scallops

PREPARATION **10 Minutes** TOTAL **20 Minutes** YIELD **6**

INGREDIENTS

- ¾ cup butter
- 3 tablespoons minced garlic
- 2 pounds large sea scallops
- 1 teaspoon salt
- 1/8 teaspoon pepper
- 2 tablespoons fresh lemon juice

DIRECTION

» Melt butter in a large skillet over medium high heat. Stir in garlic, and cook for a few seconds until fragrant, add scallops, and cook for several minutes on one side, then turn over, and continue cooking until firm and opaque. Remove scallops to a platter, then whisk salt, pepper, and lemon juice into butter. Pour sauce over scallops to serve.

Buon Appetito!

sweets

Homemade Cinnamon Rolls

PREPARATION 10 Minutes   **TOTAL** 1 hour 30 Minutes   **YIELD** 12

INGREDIENTS

Yeast
½ cup warm water

1 package active dry yeast

1 teaspoon brown sugar

Dough
1/3 cup melted coconut oil, plus more for brushing

½ cup almond milk, at room temperature

1/3 cup cane sugar

1 teaspoon sea salt

2 ¾ cups all-purpose flour, more for kneading

Filling
½ cup brown sugar

1 ½ tablespoons cinnamon

Glaze
1 ½ cups powdered sugar, sifted

3 to 4 tablespoons almond milk

½ teaspoon vanilla extract

DIRECTION

» Grease an 8x11 or 9x13-inch baking dish. In a small bowl, stir together the water, yeast, and sugar. Set aside for 5 minutes, or until the yeast is foamy. Make the dough: In a medium bowl, combine the coconut oil, almond milk, sugar, and salt. Stir in the yeast mixture. Place the flour in a large bowl, then add the yeast mixture and stir until combined. The mixture will be sticky. Use your hands to roughly knead the mixture, then turn it out onto a floured surface. Knead 3 to 4 minutes until smooth, sprinkle with more flour if needed, and form into a ball. Brush a large bowl with coconut oil and place the dough inside. Cover with plastic wrap and set aside in a warm place to rise until doubled in size, about 60 minutes.

» Make the filling :In a small bowl, mix the brown sugar and cinnamon. Punch down dough and roll out on a floured surface into a 20x14-inch rectangle. Brush with 2 tablespoons melted coconut oil and sprinkle with the cinnamon sugar to within ½ inch of the edges. Starting at one of the short 14-inch ends, roll tightly into a log, then slice into 12 rolls. Place the rolls into the baking dish, cut side up.

» Preheat the oven to 350ºF.

» Make the glaze: In a medium bowl, whisk together the powdered sugar, 3 tablespoons almond milk, and vanilla until smooth. If it's too thick, add more almond milk. Bake the rolls 25 to 30 minutes or until lightly golden on top. Remove and allow to cool for 10 minutes, then drizzle the glaze on top and serve.

Buon Appetito!

Carrot Cake Cookies

PREPARATION
20 Minutes   TOTAL
40 Minutes   YIELD
8

INGREDIENTS

1 stick butter

1 cup brown sugar

1 egg

A few drops vanilla extract

1 cup all-purpose flour

½ teaspoon of cinnamon

½ teaspoon of baking powder

½ teaspoon of baking soda

Pinch of salt

1 cup grated carrots

1 cup oats

¼ cup raisins

Cream Cheese Frosting

4 oz cream cheese

1 cup confectioner's sugar

2 tablespoons butter

Few drops vanilla

DIRECTION

» Preheat the oven to 350 F, lightly grease your cookie sheets. To make the cookie dough, combine butter and brown sugar, beat with a mixer. Add egg and vanilla, mix. In a separate bowl, combine flour, cinnamon, baking powder, baking soda and pinch of salt. Mix. Add dry ingredients to wet mixture and beat. Add carrots, oats and raisins, mix by hand. Use ice cream scooper or spoon and drop dough on to cookie sheets and bake until the edges are golden, 10 to 12 minutes. Allow the cookie to cool on the baking sheet for 1 minute before transferring to a wire rack. To make the frosting, beat the cream cheese and 2 tablespoons of butter with an electric mixer in a bowl until smooth. Add the confectioners' sugar and a few drops vanilla. Beat until no lumps remain. Spread the frosting on the cooled cookies (making sandwiches), and allow to dry completely before storing.

Buon Appetito!

Strawberry Muffins

PREPARATION
10 Minutes

TOTAL
20 Minutes

YIELD
12

INGREDIENTS

1 cup whole wheat flour

2 tablespoon truvia

¼ salt

½ baking powder

1 Cup almond milk

¼ cup egg whites

½ teaspoon vanilla

3 tablespoons apple sauce
(unsweetened)

1 tablespoon butter (melted)

1 cup strawberries (sliced)

DIRECTION

» Preheat oven to 400ºF In a large mixing bowl add flour, truvia, salt, baking powder and whisk it on up. In a small bowl whisk together egg whites, vanilla, apple sauce, butter and almond milk. Add the wet ingredients to the dry and fold in your strawberries. Grab a muffin tin and coat with non-stick cooking spray. Bake muffins for 15 minutes. Set muffins on platter and allow to cool.

Buon Appetito!

Peanut Butter Chocolate Chip Cookie Bars

PREPARATION **5 Minutes**   TOTAL **35 Minutes**   YIELD **12**

INGREDIENTS

- 2 ½ cups almond flour
- 2/3 cup peanut butter
- ¼ cup coconut oil
- ¼ cup maple syrup
- 2 teaspoons vanilla
- 1 cup Lilys Chocolate chips
- 2 tablespoons cacao powder
- 2 tablespoons water
- Pecans (optional)

DIRECTION

» Grab a baking tray and line with parchment paper. In a large bowl mix together flour, peanut butter, coconut oil, maple syrup, vanilla and chocolate chips. Add the cookie mixture to the baking tray and spread evenly. Grab a small blender and add cacao powder, water and pecans. Mix together to make a chocolate thick consistency. Add on top of the cookie mixture and spread evenly. Pop in the freezer for 30 minutes. Cut into small rectangular bars and serve.

Buon Appetito!

No Bake, No Sugar Chocolate Caramel Bites

PREPARATION 5 Minutes   **TOTAL** 10 Minutes   **YIELD** 1

INGREDIENTS

1 cup Lily's salted caramel baking chips

1 tablespoons coconut oil

Fresh walnuts (crushed)

DIRECTION

» In a double boiler pot over low heat melt the chocolate and coconut oil. Fill an ice cube tray with the chocolate mixture. Top with crushed walnuts and freeze for 30 minutes.

Buon Appetito!

Blueberry Lemon Glaze Donuts

⏱ PREPARATION **10 Minutes** ⏱ TOTAL **20 Minutes** 🍴 YIELD **6**

INGREDIENTS

1 cup all-purpose flour

2 tablespoons baking powder

1 tablespoon baking soda

½ teaspoon salt

¾ cup sugar

1 egg

3 tablespoons butter

1/3 cup almond milk

½ cup Greek yogurt

½ teaspoon vanilla

1 cup blueberries

1 cup confectioners sugar

3 tablespoons lemon juice

DIRECTION

» Preheat oven to 350°F In a large mixing bowl add flour, baking powder, baking soda, salt and sugar. In a small bowl whisk together egg, butter, milk, Greek yogurt and vanilla. Add the wet ingredients to the dry and whisk it on up. Fold in blueberries. Fill your donut tray with the batter and bake for 15 minutes. In a small bowl whisk together confectioners sugar and lemon juice. Allow donuts to cool and drizzle frosting on top.

Buon Appetito!

Edible Cookie Dough

PREPARATION
10 Minutes

YIELD
8

INGREDIENTS

3/4 smooth cup
natural peanut butter

1/3 cup melted coconut oil

1/3 cup maple syrup (sugar free)

2 teaspoons vanilla extract

3 cups almond flour

1/2 cup lilys chocolate chips

Pinch of salt

DIRECTION

» In a large bowl mix together the
peanut butter, coconut oil, maple
syrup, vanilla and salt. Add in your
almond flour and combine with all
ingredients. You may have to add a
dash of water or almond milk if the
mixture is to crumbly. Fold in your
chocolate chips. Grab a baking
sheet and line with parchment
paper. Spoon out small cookie
dough balls and store in the fridge
or freezer.

Buon Appetito!

Homemade Brownies

PREPARATION 5 Minutes | **TOTAL** 10 Minutes | **YIELD** 1

INGREDIENTS

1 ½ cups coconut sugar
¾ cup almond flour
2/3 cup cocoa powder
½ cup powdered sugar
½ cup Lily's dark chocolate chips
2 large eggs
½ cup coconut oil
½ teaspoon vanilla

DIRECTION

» Preheat the oven to 325ºF Line a baking dish with parchment paper and spray parchment with non-stick cooking spray. In a medium bowl combine sugar, flour, cocoa, powdered sugar. Chocolate chips and ½ teaspoon sea salt. In a larger bowl whisk together eggs, coconut oil, water and vanilla. Add the dry ingredients into the wet and stir until combined. Pour the batter into the baking dish and bake for 40 minutes. Allow brownies to cool, plate and serve.

Buon Appetito!

Nice Cream

PREPARATION 5 Minutes | **TOTAL** 65 Minutes | **YIELD** 4

INGREDIENTS

2 bananas (chopped up and frozen)
1 cup peanut butter
1 cup almond milk
½ cup Lily'ss Chocolate chips

DIRECTION

» Slice up bananas and freeze them for 30 minutes. Grab a blender and mix together frozen bananas, peanut butter and almond milk. Pack it into a to-go bowl and top with chocolate chips. Freeze for another 30 minutes.

Buon Appetito!

index

CPSIA information can be obtained
at www.ICGtesting.com
Printed in the USA
LVHW061514140721
692677LV00011B/572